PRAISE
THE BEER LOVER'S
GUIDE TO CIDER

"Nothing surpasses the enthusiasm and zeal of a recent convert when it comes to the desire to share a newfound passion. Cider is the lucky recipient of this in The Beer Lover's Guide to Cider, where Beth Demmon offers up numerous examples illustrating her enjoyment of the breadth of cider. Coming from a beer orientation, Beth refreshingly still wrangles with the challenges that any boundary-crossing engagement presents. There is a cider for everyone here, and this is the perfect launch pad from which to start that new adventure. Really, this is not just for beer lovers, but for everyone who wants a whole new world of drinks opened up before their eyes."

—Tom Oliver, cider maker at Oliver's Cider & Perry

"With writing and insights as crisp and lively as a freshly picked apple, Demmon takes readers to the core of today's top cider producers and deftly demonstrates how they're pressing, fermenting, and building a welcoming bridge to the world of craft beer."

—Joshua M. Bernstein, journalist and author of The Complete Beer Course

"Whether you're a beer drinker cautiously exploring new flavors or an all-around fermentation fan ready to dive in headfirst, prepare to become utterly obsessed with cider. You'll find no better copilot than Beth Demmon. She'll gently guide you through cider's history and geography while never losing sight of what's most important: how flavorful and eye-popping ciders can taste."

—Kate Bernot, director of the North American Guild of Beer Writers

"Many guides to food and drink give readers the 'what.' The best invite readers to ask, 'what if?' Demmon's Beer Lover's Guide to Cider is packed with knowledge that empowers fans of beer to explore the emergent frontier of American cider in practical, palatable terms. More significantly, Demmon invites beer drinkers to open their minds to cider as a cultural sandbox, where delighting in new sensory experiences can teach readers unexpected things about our collective history, our shared ecosystems, and the limitless power of a willing palate."

—Dr. J Jackson-Beckham, principal at Crafted For All and board member for The Michael James Jackson Foundation for Brewing & Distilling

"Recommendation-driven guides like this tend to skew on the side of navel-gazing memoirs, but Beth deftly avoids that tired territory, bringing a fresh perspective to the table instead. Her passion for cider spreads like wildfire throughout the book and her diligent research shines through as she offers just the right amount of context and objectivity to make each pick both interesting and useful. The Beer Lover's Guide to Cider is both an exciting foray into the beauty and diversity that the cider category has to offer and a must-have for beer drinkers who know what they like but seek to discover new liquid horizons."

—Emma Janzen, author of Mezcal: The History, Craft & Cocktails of the World's Ultimate Artisanal Spirit

"When it comes to food and drink, I've always found that the more you know about a thing, the more it empowers your ability to enjoy it—frame of reference counts for a lot, ultimately affecting how and what we taste. I've always been cider-curious without knowing much about it. There are few who I'd trust more than Beth Demmon to help me build that frame of reference, and I'm excited about where this book will take me."

—Joe Stange, managing editor of Craft Beer & Brewing Magazine and coauthor of Good Beer Guide Belgium

"I found Demmon's Guide to be an easy starting point for anyone—particularly craft beer lovers, homebrewers, or beer judges—interested in exploring the world of American cider and the diversity of commercial cider options available across the country. Demmon concisely and effectively packages key information about cider types and commercial cider examples to help beer lovers start to whet their palates with cider. This book will encourage anyone to develop a better appreciation for an often overlooked or misunderstood beverage."

—Dennis Mitchell, president of the Beer Judge Certification Program (BJCP)

"Beth Demmon does a fantastic job giving cider the spotlight it has long deserved. Her book is another tool that cider producers can use to convert more new, diverse, inclusive consumers into cider drinkers. She smartly uses beer as the basis of introduction to make the beverage approachable and easy to understand for those new to cider."

—Latiesha Cook, CEO, cofounder, and president of Beer Kulture

"Beth is the perfect narrator for a national tour of the modern cider landscape, and there is nobody more qualified to try hundreds of ciders and share those learnings in the vernacular that has inspired thousands to fall in love with craft breweries. In this guide, you'll find an engaging blend of her history writing for outlets coast-to-coast, from in-depth culinary and artisanal brewing coverage to entertainment. That range brings to life both the past and the present day of the American craft cider industry in these pages, leaving lessons and insights both well-timed to explore the top cider makers of our day but also timeless. Cider category tourists and craft beer lovers looking to expand their range will find education and enjoyment within."

—Bill Shufelt, cofounder of Athletic Brewing Company

"In this well-researched and clearly written guide, Beth breaks down some of the best ciders in the country into discrete categories with common characteristics and simple yet thoughtful descriptions. Despite the beer-forward title, anyone with a passing knowledge of beer and an appreciation for new beverages can rely on Beth's notable history as a judge of flavors and obviously excellent palate (she did include a couple of my ciders, after all) to steer them toward their next favorite drink."

—Nat West, president and cider maker at Reverend Nat's Hard Cider

"I'm a fan of several local cider producers here on California's Central Coast. Now here comes Beth's book to expand my horizons and bring a fresh perspective to the broader American cider scene. Any avid or budding fan of craft beverages will enjoy her unique perspective and deep dive into the world of cider, which has never been more varied and fascinating."

—Matt Brynildson, brewmaster at Firestone Walker Brewing Company

"Like many beer enthusiasts, I've never given cider too much more than a passing thought. Not anymore. As both a beer and cider expert, Beth knows exactly how to speak cider in beer language, and I for one am listening. Reading Beth's book, I not only nodded along, chuckled several times, and read numerous passages aloud to my partner, I also got urgently fired up to pull some out of the basement to see if I could apply some of her detailed sensory descriptions to what I was tasting. Complex? Funky? Delightful? What was this world I was missing? I have no doubt that beer lovers who read this book will develop a curiosity to explore cider with a newly opened mind and a sophistication that's sure to bring exuberance to their journey."

—Tara Nurin, author of A Woman's Place Is in the Brewhouse: A Forgotten History of Alewives, Brewsters, Witches, and CEOs

"Whether you're already into cider or just beginning your journey, Beth Demmon's excellent book will be the perfect guide. Eloquent, with a beautiful turn of phrase, prepare to be captivated by this explorer's companion volume. Food pairings aplenty and fascinating facts pepper the text. The sense of adventure in this fast-evolving community comes over strongly. Join them on their quest."

—Susanna Forbes, cofounder of Little Pomona Orchard & Cidery and author of The Cider Insider

"Craft beer drinkers are curious. From the earliest days of the Craft Beer Revolution, they have explored and demanded different styles and ingredients. Their curiosity flung open the door for cider, craft beer's cousin. Brewers and cider makers share a passion for innovation and creativity. While distinctive and different, we share the same store coolers and restaurant menus, and many of the same drinkers. Eleven years after the first brew of Samuel Adams Boston Lager, we introduced our first cider in 1995, and then after research and cider soul-searching, we debuted Angry Orchard in 2012. Beth Demmon followed a similar path from craft beer to cider, and we all benefit from her journey. Her knowledge and enthusiasm for craft beer and cider ennoble both beverages. The Beer Lover's Guide to Cider takes beer lovers on a wonderful journey through the cider landscape and teaches us to appreciate cider with a brewer's palate."

—Jim Koch, brewer and founder of The Boston Beer Company

"We get thousands of visitors to Virtue Farm every year, wanting to try our ciders and curious to know what makes each cider different. I'm happy to recommend Beth Demmon's new book The Beer Lover's Guide to Cider. Answering 'what's in the glass?' by style is a welcome addition to books about apples, production and history of cider. When I began brewing at Goose Island in 1988, I read Michael Jackson's World Guide to Beer cover to cover, again and again, inspiring me to explore beer. Beth's well-researched book will inspire a new generation of cider drinkers to explore the magical world of apples."

—Greg Hall, founder of Virtue Cider

THE

BEER

LOVER'S

GUIDE

TO

CIDER

THE
BEER
LOVER'S

AMERICAN CIDERS FOR
CRAFT BEER FANS
TO EXPLORE

GUIDE
TO
CIDER

BETH DEMMON

Foreword by Jeff Alworth

CORAL GABLES

For permission requests, please contact the publisher at:
Mango Publishing Group
2850 S Douglas Road, 2nd Floor
Coral Gables, FL 33134 USA
info@mango.bz

For special orders, quantity sales, course adoptions and corporate sales, please email the publisher at sales@mango.bz. For trade and wholesale sales, please contact Ingram Publisher Services at customer.service@ingramcontent.com or +1.800.509.4887.

The Beer Lover's Guide to Cider: American Ciders for Craft Beer Fans to Explore

Library of Congress Cataloging-in-Publication number: 2023937090
ISBN: (pb) 978-1-68481-240-0, (hc) 978-1-68481-417-6, (e) 978-1-68481-241-7
BISAC category code CKB111000, COOKING / Health & Healing / Gluten-Free

Printed in the United States of America

For the curious and aspiring ombibulous masses. Wassail!

Table of Contents

Foreword

 The humble apple is an amazing and versatile fruit. The tree itself is a bit of a marvel, able to grow across much of the planet and make do with many different environments. The fruit may be as small as a golf ball and tart as a lemon, or heavy and lush as a grapefruit, and sweet as candy. Most fruits come in a single, boring color, but not the apple, which may burn with the red of a hot coal or reflect the yellow of dawn sunlight. Even the inside may be creamy white or have the pinkish red of a blooming rose.

To cider makers, those differences are like paint colors to an artist. To add a bit of spice, they might select a russet, with its patchy, brown hide and vivid tannins. For structure, they include some "sharps"—apples packed with acids. They may choose another variety for its aromas, a bit of banana or pear or caramel, or perhaps geranium and rose. Much like their outsides, the insides of apples are amazingly varied. Only grapes rival apples in their complexity, and only apples and grapes can be made into a beverage with the structure, elegance, and sophistication of a wine or cider.

About twenty years ago, Americans rediscovered the apple and its capacity to make amazing fermented beverages. Taking the lead of wine and beer, small craft producers started making flavorful, complex potions. Some, taking wine as their inspiration, produced elegant, sophisticated ciders with structured acidity and earthy tannins that highlighted specific apple varieties. Others followed craft beer's example, creating expressive, improvisational ciders made with multiple fruits or hops, or which spent time aging in cast-off bourbon barrels. While mass-market ciders grabbed some attention in the middle 2010s, artisanal cider makers continued to hone their craft, and they now offer creations every bit as good as the best wines and beers on the market.

In the book you're holding, Beth Demmon acts as a guide to this world. She borrows a conceptual framework from the beer world to help you understand the flavors and aromas you'll find in cider. We build our knowledge by starting with the familiar and using it as a bridge to the unknown. In each chapter, Beth selects ciders in a particular category—like those made with hops or other fruits, or those that are tart or resemble Belgian ales. She offers specific ciders as examples, describing the flavors and ingredients as well as food pairing suggestions. As readers move through the book, they will find that bridge, moving them into territory they might have only imagined.

Before becoming our guide, Demmon was a master sleuth, finding ciders like Potter's Craft Cider's The Haven, which resembles a Belgian Abbey ale. Ciders aren't purely the products of apples, but yeast, and here she illustrates how a Belgian strain enhances the fruit. Or how about hops? This uniquely American twist is now a fixture in American cider making. Demmon takes us to Pennsylvania to try Ploughman Cider's Lummox, spiced with locally grown Citra hops. For those willing to travel even further, she suggests something more exotic, the Basque-style Garratza from Liberty Ciderworks.

Demmon is one of the most interesting writers covering the worlds of beer and cider—and their intersection. She brings a people-first approach to her storytelling, often highlighting key people standing just outside the spotlight. That perspective allows her to find the artisans doing fantastic work who have been overlooked by others. You'll find the fruit (sorry!) of her perceptive eye in these pages, where she has identified some of the country's best ciders—and not just the ones everyone knows. If you've tried cider and enjoyed it, you will find no better guide.

—Jeff Alworth

Prologue

How The Beer Lover's Guide to Cider Came to Be

I have called myself (and been called) a "craft beer nerd" since the mid-2000s. My initial interest happened to coincide with the beginning of the latest wave of beer popularity in the United States, which was preceded by the earlier peaks during the pre-Prohibition era (with over 4,000 breweries and counting in the 1870s) and the homebrew-slash-brewpub boom of the late 1970s through the mid-1990s. After a few years spent as an enthusiastic consumer of both craft beer culture and the beers themselves, I began writing professionally about the industry in 2015, became a Recognized judge through the Beer Judge Certification Program (BJCP) in 2019, and advanced to Certified in 2020, judging local, regional, and national competitions in the process. After briefly dabbling in homebrewing, I decided long ago I'd rather leave the actual creation process to the experts, but I have written about, imbibed, and evaluated thousands of beers over the years.

I wasn't properly introduced to craft cider until 2013, when one of my best friends—and also the person who initially got me into craft beer, coincidentally—began working at a small, rural cidery in Albemarle County, Virginia. He handed me a bottle of farmhouse-style dry cider, and after that first sip, I was hooked. I had no idea cider could taste like that, and I quickly realized hardly any other beer nerds did either.

"I had no idea cider could taste like that, and I quickly realized hardly any other beer nerds did either."

My transition from beer nerd to cider nerd began in earnest in 2020, when I cohosted a panel at CiderCon, the American Cider Association's (ACA) annual cider industry conference. Sitting next to wine and cider maker Pat Knittel and 2020 Pommelier of the Year Ambrosia Borowski, *Side by Side: Beer, Wine, Spirits and Cider* paired selected ciders with specific beers and wines to discuss the collective similarities and differences between them. People seemed *psyched* to have a beer voice added to the cider conversation. After connecting all of these a-ha moments, I began to grasp the unlimited potential for what American cider is today, and what it could be in the future.

I became a Certified Cider Professional through the ACA in 2021, and as soon as I began immersing myself in craft cider, the tight-knit scene immediately embraced me. Beer remains a male-dominated field, and while craft beer culture is often shown as an inclusive alternative where anyone who enjoys America's everyman beverage is welcomed equally, women; Black, Indigenous, and people of color; LGBTQ+ folks; disabled people; and other historically oppressed groups know that's often not the case. But cider, despite its overwhelming whiteness and perhaps in part to its relative fluidity of identity, seems anxious to fill their ranks with *all* newcomers. I hope it stays that way, because cider can be a great way to experience the casual camaraderie of beer culture without some of its baggage.

Despite the struggles and repressive influences American cider currently faces, which I'll detail more starting on page 23, I believe those challenges can be overcome by people with open minds and willing palates. And although there remains some pushback from those cider makers who view comparing cider to any other beverage as an unforgivable offense, the fact remains that if American cider wants to survive, they're going to have to look to the treasure trove of yet-untapped consumers.

The Beer Lover's Guide to Cider

Beer fans don't have to think too much about where their next beer is coming from. Corner stores, bodegas, supermarkets, and bottle shops carry everything from aggressively aromatic West Coast India Pale Ales (IPAs) to crisp Pilsners, mouth-puckering sours, rich and roasty Imperial Stouts, and beyond. But look for a cider on a restaurant's drinks list and you'll be lucky to find even one. It's a shame, because cider's versatility stands up to any beer, wine, or cocktail.

In the mood for something funky? Basque ciders can blow past plenty of wild fermented beers and pair fabulously with food. Looking for an after-dinner sipper without the burn? Ice cider's velvety smoothness can finish any day on a high note. Cider can be as hoppy and hazy as a New England-style IPA or as full-bodied as an Eisbock. From fruit-packed ciders in cans perfect for a summer barbecue to celebratory bottles of bubbly ready to pop amongst friends, it's time more people were introduced to the wide-ranging variety of ciders made right here in the United States.

Some curious or casual consumers don't wish to dive into the numerous (and well-documented) archives of colonial-era cider or read about the scientific properties of fermentation in order to find ciders to appreciate. If you do want to learn, plenty of cider books about all these topics already exist and I reference many of them in the Resources section on page 174. Cider fans who want a fresh perspective about the direction the US industry is heading, beer drinkers in search of something different, wine people curious about cider as an adjacent fermented fruit beverage category, or even the burgeoning class of ombibulous drinkers[1] looking to expand their minds are quite likely to uncover something new and interesting in these pages. Cider is making history, right now, so I prefer to look to the future of cider and relinquish the historical and technical analysis to others.

---

1   Drinkers who enjoy trying any and every drink, from cider to beer, spirits, wine, and beyond.

I want to know: What does American cider taste like? Where do these ciders come from? Who's making them? If you're asking yourself these same questions, you're in the right place.

"Once you cross over into the wonderful world of cider, it's hard to come back from it."

I tried every single one of the nearly 100 ciders mentioned in this book, along with hundreds more. While that number represents just a fraction of what's available across the country on any given day, the sheer span of styles, techniques, and approaches presented here proves cider has the ability to occupy a more prominent place in American consumption.

I reached out to hundreds of cideries throughout the research and sampling process. Some declined to send samples. Some ignored me. Some essentially told me to buzz off and quit contributing to the "beerification" of cider. (While their numbers are relatively few, cider trolls do exist!) Some couldn't ship to California at all or without the cost becoming prohibitively expensive. Many explained they were too small, or their products could only be acquired on-site at their rural farm. Even some producers intentionally making beer-inspired cider rotate their offerings so much that it wouldn't make sense to recommend anything that may never be made again.

This book's goal is to give drinkers a clearer glimpse of the modern American cider scene. I caution you not to consider this a "best of" list of my personal favorites, although I'd happily drink any one of these again. After years of tasting and objectively analyzing standard beer styles, this is merely a collection of ciders I believe exemplify opportunities for beer drinkers to discover familiar flavors in a brand-new beverage *and* are at least relatively accessible, either by retail distribution or direct-to-consumer shipping. This book should act as a guide to start, not finish, your own cider journey. In fact, I sincerely hope that beer and cider drinkers alike find new producers and products to seek out and try on their own. Once you cross over into the wonderful world of cider, it's hard to come back from it.

Introduction

 Cider is not beer.

In fact, there are probably more differences between the two than similarities. From the ingredients to how each is made, size of market share, and ways they're officially (and unofficially) categorized by both regulators and consumers, cider is most decidedly not beer and beer is definitely not cider.

The very notion of comparing beer and cider to one another tends to aggravate traditionalists in both camps. It's not even an apples to oranges comparison—it's apples to water, barley, yeast, and hops. The very best ciders preserve the essence of each raindrop, every sunbeam, and every pollinator that's ever landed on the fruit, which continues to evolve each and every day. Conversely, the very best beers tend to glorify the vision of their makers rather than solely focusing on the ingredients used.

Ingredients still matter immensely in beer—the best brewer is only as good as their materials—but cider's profound connection with the earth leaves it open to embrace unpredictability over consistency. If you use good apples, there's a very high chance you'll end up with good cider, or at least not bad cider. Many of the best ciders are largely left to their own devices and the whims of nature. When it comes to brewing beer, one must follow a recipe and utilize heat and mechanics. Cider making is more coaxed into existence than created or planned, as apples are plucked from trees, pressed to extract the fresh juice, left to ferment either with wild yeasts or inoculated with specific strains, and finally racked into packaging for us to drink and enjoy. In this way, cider is wine. It just uses apples rather than grapes.

Despite wine and cider's more numerous similarities, connections do exist between the beer and cider worlds. If wine and cider are siblings, beer and cider are more like second cousins once removed. These bridges between the beverages—some obvious, some more abstract—mean those accustomed to reaching for a cold beer may be shocked to develop a newfound appreciation for cider. From recognizable flavors and a laid-back culture to a diversity of styles, mouthfeel, and food pairings, cider isn't just an alternative to those tired of drinking beer or who seek a gluten-free alcohol option. It's a class in itself, worthy of appreciation and exploration. But considering how small cider is today in the United States, it hasn't yet crossed many people's minds to even try cider or know where to start.

Beer isn't better than cider. It's just a lot bigger. It's also way, way easier to find, from grocery store shelves to the approximately 9,500 breweries and taprooms across the United States.[2] Comparatively, as of 2023, there are an estimated 1,700 cider producers,[3] with just a handful of cider-centric bars left in the entire country. The nation's top beer producers churn out millions of barrels of beer annually, while one company dominates around half of the entire American cider market: Angry Orchard. Angry Orchard falls under the Boston Beer Company family of brands, which also includes Samuel Adams, Dogfish Head Craft Brewery, Truly Hard Seltzer, and Twisted Tea. Big Cider literally exists because of beer.

If measured against the size of the US beer market, American cider would occupy around one percent. Even the craft beer segment makes up more than

---

2   According to the Brewers Association, https://www.brewersassociation.org/year-in-beer. For comparison's sake, 20 years ago there were fewer than 1,500 breweries and taprooms in operation across the United States.

3   According to IBISWorld, https://www.ibisworld.com/industry-statistics/number-of-businesses/cider-production-united-states/

10 times that amount.[4] Apples are one of the top five fruits most consumed by Americans today.[5] We just aren't drinking them that much. People have been predicting cider's sudden rise for years now, yet it seems to have stalled on the cusp for a tiringly long time. For cider to finally rise to its potential, several barriers must first be overcome.

- **We have yet to define what cider is.** When I say cider, I'm referring to the alcoholic drink made from the fermented juice of apples. "Hard cider" is redundant—no one says "hard wine." "Soft cider" is non-fermented apple juice, a perennial childhood favorite. And we haven't even gotten into the jumbled vocabulary of the cider industry itself, who use terms like craft cider, heritage cider, and heirloom cider without a universally agreed upon definition for any of them. People don't even agree on what "cider apple" means. Sometimes it means apples that are too hard or too soft to eat, but can be used for cider. Sometimes it means apples specifically grown to be made into cider. Cider hasn't figured itself out yet, and newcomers aren't going to do it for them.

- **Most people still think all cider is sweet.** That's because for a long time, and for a lot of commercially available ciders, this was true. The only stuff relatively available to *most* people at *most* stores was back-sweetened alco-pops with apple aroma added. As more local and regional cideries expand their distribution, that reputation is changing, but it's hard to persuade people who think they've already tried all that cider has to offer and didn't like it. Today, I wager that the vast majority of Americans don't have a clue about the actual breadth of domestic cider and haven't yet been convinced to give it a real chance.

---

4 According to the Brewers Association's National Beer Sales & Production Data, https://www. brewersassociation.org/statistics-and-data/national-beer-stats/
5 According to Statista and the US Department of Agriculture.

- **Rules and regulations have stifled cider's growth.** Two different government agencies oversee wine (and thus, cider), depending on the alcohol content. Any cider over 7.0 percent alcohol-by-volume (ABV) falls under the jurisdiction of the Alcohol and Tobacco Tax and Trade Bureau (TTB). Any cider below 7.0 percent ABV is regulated by the United States Food and Drug Administration (FDA). Their regulations are similar, but not identical, and that's not even getting into the three-tier system's disparate—and often arbitrary—enforcement between segments, complicated federal excise tax laws for ciders over 8.5 percent ABV, a varying tax structure for ciders that contain added fruit or high carbonation, or prohibitions against things like listing the year of harvest. Cider's hands are tied by red tape, and despite the industry rallying for change, it remains irritatingly at the mercy of a capitalistic bureaucracy.

- **Cider has done a bad job promoting itself.** Much of what's been written about American cider focuses on the drink's heyday from the late 1700s to the early 1900s, preferring to wax nostalgic about this glorious past rather than create a new future. But now that cider has an opportunity to define itself anew, it must find the ability to approach, attract, and appeal to more people to actually grow. Not only do many people simply not think about cider as a purchasing option, many of those who are aware of cider have already brushed it off or don't value it in the same realm as beer, wine, or spirits. When it comes to people with Celiac disease or who subscribe to a gluten-free or gluten-reduced diet and still want to drink alcohol, cider remains an easy, affordable, and yet underutilized go-to, but most people aren't passively discovering cider for themselves. When there are two pages of beer, four pages of wine, and six pages of spirits or cocktails on a menu, and maybe one or two cider options at best, getting into cider isn't going to just happen accidentally.

"Cider can take the best parts of craft beer—the romance of its creation, an appreciation of artistry, a supportive community, and curiosity of discovery—to become the biggest and best version of itself."

By proactively seeking out consumers to educate them about the reality of cider, as well as empowering them to explore this segment with fresh eyes, there's no reason the cider industry can't once again fulfill its legacy as the American drink of choice. People are ready for change—in fact, drinking habits are shifting by the day. Compared to Millennials, Gen Xers, Boomers, and older generations, Generation Z and even younger consumers of legal drinking age are more interested in flavor and variety than base spirit. Other high value conversion points include an increased demand for low sugar and gluten-free options, locally sourced and eco-friendly products, and a wide range of pricing: all of which cider offers.

Cider also has a unique opportunity to learn from craft beer's successes and failures. Craft beer's skyrocketing trajectory has cooled in recent years, due to factors like an overabundance of competition, supply chain shortages, and a decrease in segment-loyal consumers. It has also in many ways become a parody of itself, succumbing to the same elitist culture it touted itself as an exception to. Cider can take the best parts of craft beer—the romance of its creation, an appreciation of artistry, a supportive community, and curiosity of discovery—to become the biggest and best version of itself.

A Few Things to Know About American Cider

For a long time, American cider's sticky-sweet stereotype was not too far off from the truth. The lion's share of the industry continues to be dominated by one maker: Angry Orchard. With their staggering dominion over the entire US cider market, they're often the first (and occasionally last) cider consumers come across. Many of their products land closer to sweet than dry, so with market control of that magnitude, it's no wonder people think *all* cider is the same.

But craft cideries are quietly beginning to challenge Goliath. In 2013, estimates showed just over 300 commercial cideries across the United States. Ten years later, that number has grown to nearly six times that number, with cideries now in all 50 states and Washington, DC. Small and regional cideries dictate much of this growth, cutting into what was once a near monopoly.

But Big Cider isn't the only thing stifling craft cider. Beer is actually one of the reasons cider originally faced a decline in the US. In the mid- to late-1800s, German immigrants sparked a new brewing industry to bring their favorite beverages from their homelands to their new country. At the same time, industrialization made brewing beer easier than ever, increasing supply and in turn, sparking demand. Cider's homespun story and seasonal production window make for a romantic anecdote, but not so much immediate accessibility or consistent product. Thanks to free two-day shipping and global supply chains, American appetites for quick and easy have only grown. Even lager breweries struggle with the perceived "extra" time it takes. Multiply that time by years and you've got cider: a delicious but persnickety product people have to wait to get and one that changes batch to batch.

Although the current wave of American cider is still teetering on the brink of advancement, it has taken strides that beer has yet to take. Women and men tend to make and drink cider in roughly equal numbers. While the vast majority of cider makers are white, the Black community makes up a huge number of cider consumers and are beginning to tap into ownership and production as well. Hannah Ferguson made history as the first Black woman brewer and the first Black woman cider maker in the state of Ohio, opening D.O.P.E. Cider House & Winery in 2022. In 2016, Brooklyn Brewery brewmaster Garrett Oliver collaborated with renowned British cider maker Tom Oliver and Thornbridge Brewery to create one of the earliest crossovers between beer and cider: The Serpent, a 10.0 percent ABV Belgian Golden Ale refermented with cider *lees*[6] over 18 months in bourbon barrels. After seeing a disparity between white makers and Black attendees at a cider festival, Ashley Johnson and Jasmine Mason decided to launch The Cider Jawns to embrace, educate, and empower other Black consumers to learn more about the developing American cider scene.

These are just a few examples of the forward-thinking and inclusive nature cider is rebuilding from the ground up. Beer, on the other hand, must significantly course-correct in order to stifle its decline, as many non-white, non-male consumers begin to trickle away from machismo culture. Cider must still grapple with its whitewashed folklore, such as the near erasure of James Madison Ruffin, a formerly enslaved and eventually emancipated gardener who, along with his family, oversaw Appomattox Manor's plantation and cider making facilities during the Civil War era.[7] Other corrections include dismantling the legacy of Thomas Jefferson's orchards, whose success should actually be credited to enslaved people like Jupiter Evans,[8] who also ran his cider operations and has been honored by modern day cider makers such as Meriwether Cider and Albemarle CiderWorks, as well as George and

---

6 Residual yeast sediment left over after fermentation.

7 *Slavery and the Underground Railroad at the Eppes Plantation*, a Special Historical Study by Marie Tyler-McGraw under the Cooperative Agreement between the National Park Service and the Organization of American Historians, 2005.

8 *American Cider in Black and White*, by Olivia Maki for Civil Eats (May 10, 2019).

Ursula Granger[9] and countless other Black women and men whose stories have been nearly lost, but whose impact is still felt and not forgotten.

Beer, wine, and indeed the majority of American industries are all guilty of rewriting history to erase and minimize the efforts of Indigenous groups, enslaved Black people, and immigrants and refugees, but cider now has a unique opportunity to honor its past in order to build a better future. You don't have to know any of this to start drinking and enjoying cider. If your ultimate goal is to appreciate American cider in its entirety, understanding the context of past, present, and future can help to inform your experience. But one inescapable aspect you must understand before you can start truly appreciating cider is apples.

When it comes to beer, brewers select certain yeasts, malts, and hop varieties for their unique characteristics and how they combine for aromatics, bittering, or particular flavors. Cider follows a similar mindset, but with different apple varieties, which are separated into four categories:

Sweet: containing low acid and low tannin. Examples include Fuji, Roxbury Russet, Honeycrisp, Golden Delicious, and Gala.

Sharp: containing high acid and low tannin. Examples include Gravenstein, Granny Smith, Ashmead's Kernel, Winesap, and McIntosh.

Bittersweet: containing low acid and high tannin. Examples include Dabinett, Bulmer's Norman, Yarlington Mill, and Tremlett's Bitter.

Bittersharp: containing high acid and high tannin. Examples include Kingston Black, Hewe's Crab, Porter's Perfection, and Stoke Red.

---

9 *George and Ursula Granger: The Erasure of Enslaved Black Cidermakers*, by Darlene Hayes for Cider Culture (February 9, 2022), originally published in *Malus* (Issue 13, 2021).

Acid tends to make other flavors and sweetness pop, while tannins can impart and accentuate astringency through mouthfeel and occasionally a bittering element to balance against sweetness, both residual and perceived. It also affects the color of cider—when an apple's flesh is exposed to oxygen, it turns brown. In general, the more tannins an apple contains, the darker the cider containing that apple can become.

Acidity and tannins aren't typically used as primary beer descriptors in an official judging capacity or even casual tasting notes (other than alpha acids, the main bittering agents in hops). Still, understanding the interplay between them and the fermentable sugars within apples will help you understand how certain cider makers use single varieties and blends to create balance, the ultimate feature of many craft ciders. Not all American cider makers aim for balance, but with practice, you'll be able to differentiate between *good* cider and *great* cider.

How to Talk About & Taste Cider

While not everyone subscribes to BJCP style guidelines, they're widely accepted as the standard by which most beer styles are categorized and judged. In cider, different competitions use different guidelines, as well as cider style guides individually spelled out by the ACA and BJCP. American cider has yet to agree on many universal styles or definitions—in short, cider hasn't had its Michael J. Jackson moment.[10] But with that floundering comes flexibility and the opportunity to begin enjoying cider without second-guessing oneself. Creating styles helps bind us together in a shared

---

10 As one of the most influential beer writers in history, Jackson's *The World Guide to Beer* (Courage, 1977) largely developed the lexicon of modern beer styles as we know them today.

understanding, but beware of subscribing to them too deeply, lest those bonds become shackles.

Tasting cider, in my experience, is more difficult than tasting beer. Cider's essence remains nuanced and ever-changing not only in each batch, but many times in each bottle or even each sip. These subtleties can't easily be replicated, nor do many makers wish to do so. Regardless, I hope you take this challenge as an invitation rather than a deterrent.

Here's something most people won't tell you is actually okay: You can start with "It tastes good" or "It tastes bad" before getting more specific. It's fine to build up from an immediate reaction. It's just not going to help you very much if you stop there. Saying "Cider tastes like apples" echoes the same tired claim that "beer-flavored beer" is something that exists. Go deeper. Does it taste like a green, yellow, or red apple you've tried before? Does it feel sharp on your tongue or soft on the palate? If floral notes pop out, are they more lavender or jasmine? Where would you drink this: next to a roaring bonfire on a camping trip, on a picnic blanket surrounded by spring daisies, or poolside during a summertime barbecue?

The process of beginning to understand the complexities of what many consider to be a "simple" drink isn't too far off from any deductive tasting procedure, like the Court of Master Sommeliers tasting grid or BJCP score sheets. Start with appearance: What does the cider look like? What color is it? Are there a lot of bubbles or very few? Does it slowly slink down the sides of a glass viscously or swish cleanly from side to side? Can you see through it or is it cloudy?

Where's the head?

Beer fans may notice a lack of a thick, foamy, long-lasting head after pouring a cider. Since cider doesn't contain malt, this is scientifically normal and not indicative of any flaw. Having no malt also means cider is naturally gluten-free, which can be a huge benefit for anyone looking to reduce or eliminate gluten from their diet.

Moving to aromatics, give it a swirl and a whiff. Is there anything immediately off about the scent, or does it draw you in? If the cider is poured into a glass, does it allow the aromatics to breathe freely or are they muffled? How intense is the aroma and what can you draw out of it? Is it fruity, herbal, spicy, floral, or earthy? Do you detect wood character from a barrel, or minerality from water or soil? You can (and should) also revisit the aroma to see how it changes over time and as it warms.

Time to start exploring flavor and mouthfeel.[11] Does the cider fill your mouth and linger heavily on your tongue, or does it slide quickly and crisply down your throat? How does the flavor relate to the aroma—is it equal in intensity, or does one seem stronger than the other? Does it taste subtle and straightforward, or are there levels of flavor that reveal themselves over time? Does the serving temperature seem too cold, too warm, or just right to accentuate the components? Are there any discernible off-flavors? If it tastes "fruity," is it something like a ripe banana or more like a sharp quince? If it's sour, is it like vinegar or lemon? Is the finish sweet, dry, or somewhere in between? Cider's carbonation ranges from still (not carbonated) to sparkling (ultra-bubbly), so how carbonated is it, and how does that affect the way you experience how it tastes and feels?

The more practice you have drinking cider, and the more experience you can draw from comparing it to other beverages like beer, spirits, and wine, the easier it will be for you to flip through a mental notepad of tasting notes as you advance your cider proficiency.

---

11 In general, cider's mouthfeel tends to be lighter than many beer styles, depending on the level of tannins and carbonation.

Much of the existing vocabulary of beer and wine tasting remains woefully Eurocentric, leaving out fruits, vegetables, herbs, and other flavor tie-ins from outside the Westernized world. People in Japan, Chile, Denmark, and Ethiopia could all drink the same beverage and describe it in completely different terms, each shaped by unique cultural influences and traditional ingredients and cuisines. If we're able to apply our country's history of embracing flavors from around the world, cider has the potential to implement the most wide-reaching vocabulary of any beverage segment to date.

Tasting guides are merely that: guides for starting to build a framework for your own understanding. However, they are neither canon nor static. (For the most part—there are certain baselines outside subjective opinion, such as level of carbonation or color.) I once had a highly ranked BJCP beer judge tell me "wet dog" wasn't a universal enough descriptor for everyone to understand. (We eventually agreed to disagree.) I say, what's so important about making a universal diagnosis? My "wet dog" may be another person's "mildewy socks" or "rotten banana hidden by a two-year-old for a month in the corner of a closet covered in dirty laundry and cat hair" (a completely hypothetical aroma, of course). If there's enough information there to inspire you to unpack your own perceptions drawn from your own experiences, then that's a start. Treat descriptors as the beginning, not the end, and by the last chapter of this book, you'll be able to taste cider as cider and not simply an alternative to beer.

If you find flavor wheels useful, by all means utilize them. But if you prefer to wax poetic and describe cider as "sun-dappled ripe strawberries picked from a garden hothouse along a river's edge with the light touch of a summer's breeze," please do so! It's certainly not wrong, and it evokes a brighter mental image for people to share rather than "tastes like strawberry jelly." If someone does tell you that you're tasting something "wrong," there's a 99 percent chance they're a pretentious know-it-all. There's no such thing as tasting something wrong. Trust your palate. It's yours and only yours.

Beverage enthusiasts and makers tend to forget that the vast majority of everyday people have no idea what we're talking about. In the grand scheme of life, very few people could explain the difference between Ale and Lager, much less techniques like decoction mash, terms like acetaldehyde, or even what esters are. Caught up in our own circles of expertise, we expect everyone to know what we know, and there's little incentive for people to learn more when they're met with derisive snobbery or a surprise quiz about what they're drinking. Humans are only beginning to scratch the surface of expressing what taste actually is.

"There's no such thing as tasting something wrong."

Cider is no different, except in that cider has yet to develop the same number of rules as other segments (and there are currently fewer people to argue with). The ACA and BJCP's guidelines for cider can be very helpful for creating structure for personal understanding and judging criteria. However, rigid categorization of styles at such an early stage of industry development runs the risk of curbing innovation. I don't anticipate pros-and-cons debate about guidelines to settle down anytime soon, but at the heart of it, sharing vocabulary and experience remains at the heart of building a growing culture of appreciation, understanding, and community.

How to Start Pairing Cider with Food

Just as cider can and should be appreciated as an art form in its own right, so can it be appreciated by itself. Nonetheless, an easy way to start appreciating cider is by pairing it with food. I believe cider's flexibility makes it the best beverage to pair with food, including beer, and yes, wine.

The four foundational pairing methods are known as the "Four C's." They are:

Complement: Pairing "like with like" in both flavor and heft or texture. Sweet ciders can go well with desserts or other similarly sweet foods in the same way that a cider with strawberries in it can pop alongside a salad tossed with strawberries, spinach, feta, and almonds. Light ciders can work with light fare, just as richer ciders with a heavier mouthfeel can stand up against hearty dishes like roasts or baked ziti.

Contrast: Instead of like with like, this method instead aims to use opposing characteristics in food and cider in order to harmoniously highlight the differences between the two. For example, try pairing a cider made with apples containing high levels of tannins against a high acid food, such as lemon bars or tomato sauce. This approach can take some practice to avoid overpowering one or the other.

Cut: Thanks to cider's inherent ability to direct one's palate without dominating, I find this to be one of the most fulfilling and exciting ways to pair cider with food. A hopped cider with a crisp mouthfeel and refreshing finish can accentuate spicy food's depth while also cutting through the pain (or pleasure, depending on your spice tolerance). Well-carbonated ciders can also cleanse your palate, creating a blank slate with each sip upon which to thoroughly enjoy every bite of a meal.

Complete: Artisanal cider's ultimate goal is balance, so there's not always a missing element to be filled with food. With that in mind, instead of thinking of how to complete the cider, I find this method works best when starting with the food itself. Unfussy and unadorned foods made with high-quality ingredients can be majestic in their simplicity, but when paired with a complex cider exploding with acid, tannins, fermentation personality, or even additional ingredients like spices, fruits, or herbs, achieving completion is akin to achieving enlightenment.

These aren't the only ways to pair cider with food by any means, but they are effective starting points. Another framework to consider is more geographically inclined, or "What grows together, goes together." Try pairing food from a certain farm with ciders made with apples grown on the same farm or in the same region to savor the terroir of different areas across the country and world.

I finally said it: the T word. I don't think anyone should be afraid of the word terroir. It literally means the sense of a place, and isn't necessarily tied to the flavor of something, though it can be. Terroir consists of distinct personality traits, uniquely developed by nature, that only reveal themselves to those paying attention. It's less about the science of pairing and more about the artistry.

The main thing to remember when beginning to pair food with cider is that nothing you do is wrong. There aren't actually any hard-and-fast rules other than your own preferences. If—and when—you're ready to broaden your perspective of flavors, I encourage you to break out of the "traditional" model of food pairing that remains stubbornly Eurocentric, as discussed previously. Pairing cider with cheese and charcuterie is easy. But have you tried it with Vietnamese, Nordic, or Cuban dishes? The United States is known for its diversity of cuisines, so take advantage. If you're reading this, you're probably ready to expand your drinking horizons, so you might as well expand your culinary horizons at the same time. Pairing based on proximity is just as legitimate as looking outside our own invisible borders for fresh inspiration, so see what speaks to you on a particular day and play around. It's impossible to fail.

When it's time to start buying ciders either to pair or drink by themselves, a common refrain in cider circles is "The best place to drink cider is where the apples are grown." Idealistically, that's true. It's an indescribable experience to hold an apple in your hand and know the cider in your glass came directly from that. However, orchards mainly occupy regions with cold winters and plenty of sunshine: namely, places like Washington, New York, Michigan, Pennsylvania, Oregon, and Virginia. Cideries aren't exclusively limited to the farms where the apples grow, so no matter where you live in the US, there's some level of cider accessibility. It's as naïve to expect an aspiring cider drinker to fly to the Finger Lakes of New York to learn about cider as it would be to suggest that a wine novice should begin in Bordeaux. In reality, the best place to start finding cider is where you can actually find it. Scour your local bottle shops, wine bars, and when possible, local cider makers. Order a flight and see what stands out. Bring a bottle of cider instead of a six-pack of beer for your next party. Keep an open mind.

I can't tell you what you're going to like or hate, and every cider and pairing listed within these pages is subjective. If you disagree with me on these recommendations, that's actually a *good* thing. It means that you're beginning to be aware of your own palate and its differences to others. Argue with me, but try everything. Listen to your instincts and trust yourself. And, of course, have fun—responsibly and in moderation. Cider is only fun if you're alive to taste it. Are you ready to make the leap?

Introductory Ciders

01

Alternatives to Pilsners, Kölsches, American Light Lagers, Cream Ales, and Other Easy-Drinking Beers

The first beer I remember ever trying was Miller Lite, which is probably the same first beer for 92.4736 percent of Americans. As a longtime craft beer drinker and journalist, there's a lot to criticize about macro Lagers and the global conglomerates that make them. But as an observer recording the fermented beverage industry's operations, the ability to consistently churn out gobsmacking volumes of liquid that tastes virtually identical to every other batch before it is astounding. (And let's be honest, even the most hardcore believers in "craft" pick up a 12-pack of the mass-produced stuff every once in a while.)

With cider, consistency is not the point, but ease of enjoyment is. A single scrambled egg prepared perfectly can be as masterful as the trickiest soufflé, and when it comes to introductory beers as well as ciders, there's little for the maker to hide behind. In future chapters, we'll dive into ciders that take a different approach to complexity—not better or worse, just different.

All but one of these ciders come in cans rather than glass bottles, which is less coincidental as it is inevitable when marketing to beer drinkers. Exposure to ultraviolet light can affect flavor, but over time, so can aluminum. Some cider makers avoid cans altogether, while others embrace it for its versatility and convenience. For the beginning cider drinker, I recommend focusing less on the packaging and more on the product within.

The beginning and end of longtime fermented beverage consumers' preferences tend to look similar: accessible, approachable, easygoing beverages that aim to satisfy rather than challenge. When getting into a new segment, people generally reach first for what they can afford and what they can easily find before deciding to wait in line for a hype release or blow a bonus check on a single bottle. Extreme beer geeks linger at the crest of the curve, getting deep into trading, planning trips solely to visit breweries, and actively using check-in apps and message boards as craft beer continues to dominate their entire lives. However, the pendulum always swings back, and with a maturation of a craft beer palate comes a taste for simplicity, opting for a well-made Cream Ale rather than a Quadruple IPA with a laundry list of adjuncts.

The ciders in this chapter are easy and unassuming—an ideal place for the cider novice to start building a foundation of appreciation. These are to accompany you while gardening, or to put in the communal cooler at the neighborhood barbecue. These can be the first drink after working out. These are the ciders you can drink without thinking too hard about, but *should* you decide to pay attention, you are very likely to be rewarded with delight.

Shacksbury // Classic
Vergennes, Vermont | 5.2%

Shacksbury has arguably done more than any other small American cider producer to bring craft cider into the beer world. Others have certainly done their fair share—Greg Hall at Virtue Cider in Fennville, Michigan, and Nat West from Reverend Nat's Hard Cider in Portland, Oregon, come to mind—but Shacksbury's mix of eye-catching branding, brewery collaborations, and generally approachable styles distributed across the United States make it an ideal place for the cider-curious to start.

Classic is less of a replacement for light-bodied and well-attenuated beers like Czech Lagers and Kölsches and more of an alternative in terms of crispness, moderate carbonation, and understated flavor characteristics. Shacksbury calls Classic "the gold standard for a classic dry cider," and it would be pretentious if it weren't true. Thanks to it being in a can, you can bring it to most places. You can count on it tasting very similar, if not the same, from batch to batch. Its round mouthfeel, soft finish, light body, and balanced flavor provide a fairly easy bridge for anyone looking to leap from beer to cider. Stash a few in the communal cooler at your next cookout and see who you (pleasantly) surprise.

Food Pairings

Classic provides a subtle palette for your palate without any fuss and frills to distract from what's on your plate. From burgers and potato salad to chips and dip, hot dogs, fried chicken, and other classic cookout fare, this extraordinarily accessible cider is a great addition to any meal, but especially ones shared with friends.

Artifact Cider Project // Slow Down
Cambridge and Florence, Massachusetts | 6.0%

It's easy to be seduced by the big, bold flavors American craft beer tends to define itself with, but don't mistake cider's simplicity as boring. For **Slow Down**, Artifact used solely locally grown McIntosh apples and let them wild ferment to eventually become a moderately carbonated and light-bodied cider that finishes dry and refreshing.

Artifact's ciders all seem to have a shared soul from a house yeast strain, imparting a very specific, very discreet light funk throughout each one. But Slow Down is far from anything I'd call "funky." There's a light minerality balanced with a dash of citrus essence that, when observed, brings a complexity that can stop you in your tracks in order to ponder its origin. Artifact describes Slow Down's vibe as "pause button," which seems apt.

One of the big differences between cider and beer is how acids and tannins express themselves, and Slow Down is a great place to start playing around with your understanding of both. Plus, this relatively acidic, bubbly, and smooth cider perfectly encapsulates the "Cut" approach to food pairing. Crack a can during your next pizza night, or consider bringing a few to the holiday table instead of chilled white wine. For a more complementary pairing, Slow Down truly sings alongside oysters: preferably raw, but grilled if so desired.

Food Pairings & Additional Recommendations

Long Way Back and **Feels Like Home** are two other Artifact creations with the potential to convert beer drinkers to cider drinkers. Long Way Back is closer to balanced than dry or sweet, with more personality than a Lager. Feels Like Home is what I call a lawn mower beer, best enjoyed with a bit of sweat on your brow and with a bag of jalapeño kettle chips (or, if you're lucky, some Chesapeake Bay crab chips).

The Beer Lover's Guide to Cider

Dwinell Country Ales // Forrest
Goldendale, Washington | 6.7%

 Dabbling in both beer and cider, Dwinell Country Ales blurs the lines between both with harmonious results. In a sea of standouts, **Forrest** goes beyond mere greatness and enters the realm of the exceptional. High acid apples spontaneously fermented to dry coalesce together to create a *pétillant naturel* (pét-nat)[12] cider made with a blend of Jonathan, Winesap, Roxbury Russet, and Braeburn apples from E.Z. Orchards in Salem, Oregon, and pressed at Eola Hills Winery in the Willamette Valley.

Expect quite a bit of effervescent activity when opening, but Forrest tends to quickly calm itself for easy, if not somewhat lively, pouring. This pale yellow liquid with a hint of haze almost seems tinged with a bit of frost—a shade that I imagine one might witness from a slowly melting snowpack flowing into a mountain stream. Its intriguing appearance is matched with aromatic complexity that ranges from floral to fresh grass with a delicate minerality, evoking a vision of a pastoral panorama painted by one of the great landscape painters. Forrest is what the land tastes like, neither sour nor stationary, merely capturing both its ever-changing complexity as well as timeless presence.

Beer lovers will find it easy to ponder the craftsmanship of this cider. It's not one that aims to fool a drinker into thinking this could be a beer; rather, it's an option for those who seek poetry in a glass. The similarities here come from a crisp finish, high carbonation, and complexity that remains accessible to anyone dedicated to artistic expression.

---

12 Translated from French, *pétillant naturel* means "naturally sparkling." Pét-nat wines and ciders are made using the *méthode ancestral* process, in which the liquid is bottled before primary fermentation is complete and no additional yeast or sugar is added. This results in a well-carbonated, low sugar, low-to-moderate ABV product generally meant to be drunk fresh.

Food Pairings

Forrest stands by itself, so when pairing with this particular cider, I encourage restraint to avoid overpowering your palate. A goat cheese spread on crackers or a quiche with springtime vegetables would work well here, as would carrots or herbs snipped from a home garden. Anything simple, fresh, and from the earth is encouraged.

ANXO Cider // Transcontinental
Washington, DC | 6.9%

 Walk into any Lager brewery and you'll likely catch at least a faint whiff of sulfur. If your eyes start burning from a burnt match stench or your gag reflex goes into overdrive because it reeks of rotten eggs, rest assured that is not normal, correct, or acceptable, and you should probably run. However, a subtle sulfuric note on the nose of a beverage can actually add a lovely dimension to certain styles, especially on beers like German Pilsners or certain English brews that can sometimes emit yeast-derived, sulfuric-tinged aromatics that dissipate quickly.

Using English bittersweet apples from the Pacific Northwest alongside Virginia-grown GoldRushes, **Transcontinental** evokes similar aromatics to those in German Pilsners with an initially soft and pleasant sulfur scent that quickly gives way to fresh, juicy apple. This highly carbonated cider contains plenty of tannins, boosted in part by ANXO's use of wine yeast, and finishes quite dry. However, they manage to balance the crispness with a soft mouthfeel, creating a perfect marriage of cider tradition with modern accessibility. In this case, Transcontinental doesn't just bridge a continent; it unites two completely different but equally delightful beverage segments, and has the potential to surprise fans of both.

About ANXO Cider

ANXO's collaborations with and imports from iconic European craft cider producers like Little Pomona Orchard & Cidery, Oliver's Cider & Perry, and Ross-on-Wye Cider & Perry Company have opened the door for drinkers in the United States to be able to experience some of the world's best ciders without having to fly across the Atlantic. With this access to the pioneers of modern cider, American drinkers have the privilege of selecting either local favorites *or* acclaimed ciders from abroad: a win-win for cider explorers.

Golden State Cider // Brut
Sonoma County, California | 6.9%

If Japanese Lagers are beer's answer to Champagne, **Brut** is a strong contender on the cider side. It's no surprise why—this desiccatingly dry drink uses Champagne yeast to ferment apples grown on the West Coast, resulting in a light yellow, mostly clear, extremely bubbly beverage with nary a sugar molecule remaining.

So if there's no sugar and no gluten, what's left? A lip-smackingly dry cider that provides a glimpse into what apple flavor can be when whittled to its very essence. The Champagne yeast works overtime to help make this juice shine, and the beauty lies within its simplicity. Mistakes have nowhere to hide, and good luck finding something wrong with Brut.

This particular option from Golden State Cider can certainly be a celebratory alternative for special occasions, but its tall can format lends it a less precious aura than a bottle waiting to be popped. That's not to say it won't turn heads. Most Brut cans I've cracked open are about as loud as cans get without exploding, so this is a solid, affordable, no-sugar option to consider instead of another cheap bottle of mediocre bubbly.

Additional Recommendation

Both Brut and **Mighty Dry** are bright and effervescent options for beginner cider drinkers as well as those further along on their cider journeys. Both are relatively easy to acquire, thanks to their wide distribution network along the West Coast as well as direct-to-consumer shipping options across the country. Mighty Dry is a smidge lower in alcohol content (6.3 percent) and retains a bit more rounded apple personality, but frankly, the reliable consistency of both makes them refreshing options to elevate pairings or to simply practice cider tasting.

Yonder Cider // Sunnyslope
Wenatchee and Seattle, Washington | 6.9%

 It's time to rethink brunch, and **Sunnyslope** can help. This pink grapefruit and lemon verbena cider is Yonder's take on a Greyhound, the pre-Prohibition era cocktail typically made with grapefruit juice and either vodka or gin. In Greyhounds, the spirit cuts through citrus tartness to provide balance, but in Sunnyslope, balance comes from its dry finish, bright fruit acidity, and floral aromatics. Using a blend of Fuji, Honeycrisp, Pink Lady, Granny Smith, Roxbury Russet, and other bittersharp apples, Sunnyslope melds into a light and crisp cider ideal for a Shandy or a brunch beverage alternative.

Sunnyslope can be more than an easy-drinking Sunday morning cider. Since it is citrus-forward, it also pairs well with savory snacks like Castelvetrano olives, a spicy mixed nut medley, or an assortment of dry cheeses and charcuterie. Bring a pack of Sunnyslope to your next potluck or dinner party and experiment with how the bright flavors can liven up an evening just as well as they can start the day.

How to Mix Sunnyslope

Mixing cider with beer or spirits is a great way to experience cider's versatility. Thanks to Sunnyslope's lemon and grapefruit backbone, it mixes particularly well with tequila for a fresh take on a Tequila Sunrise, which Yonder calls a "Yonder Sunrise." You'll need three ounces of Sunnyslope, one ounce of tequila (I recommend blanco tequila), and one-quarter ounce of triple sec. Build over ice and swizzle, then serve in a Collins glass.

For a cider twist on a summer Shandy, the variations are endless. Try mixing Sunnyslope with your preferred Pilsner, Wheat Beer, or Lager and see what works. The proportion can be two-thirds beer to one-third cider, half and half, or any combination you fancy. The best part is it's impossible to mess up, so experiment away!

Sincere Cider // Apple Dry Cider
Napa, California | 5.6%

 Sincere Cider doesn't make lots of different products, choosing instead to focus on perfecting a small number of apple-driven ciders. The result is a handful of interesting and bright 16-ounce cans with eye-catching geometric designs that look just at home on beer shelves as they do in the cider and wine sections. In fact, if it weren't for the prominent apple pattern on the can, you'd be forgiven for mistaking **Apple Dry Cider** as beer at first glance.

One sip in and it's clear this is no beer. What it is, however, is an ode to springtime, with aromatics ranging from fresh linen to apple blossoms and a juicy finish inviting sip after sip. The mostly dry finish and light body are balanced with just the barest hint of acid and tartness to remind drinkers that yes, this is made with fruit. Sincere only uses fresh-pressed apple juice from culinary apples grown in Washington State, and with just five grams of sugar per can, Sincere owner Bex Pezzullo calls this a "fully crushable" and sessionable alternative for those looking for something fun, delicious, and new.

About Sincere Cider

Sincere Cider is one of the few queer- and women-owned cider companies in the United States, making them part of the one percent of the one percent. Regardless of personal opinion, food and drinks are political, and greater diversity in the boardroom and beyond is a boon for all humanity. Plus, as a member of 1% For The Planet, Sincere directly donates a minimum of one percent of all sales to environmentally focused nonprofits. With unshakeable tenets of equity, inclusion, and sustainability at Sincere's core, their success makes this cidery a bellwether for American cider.

Austin Eastciders // Texas Brut
Austin, Texas | 4.2%

 Texas Brut incorporates a comfortingly familiar light body, moderate carbonation, mild aromatics, and very dry finish—all the ease of a Light Lager, boosted with a splash of fruit oomph. Austin Eastciders isn't shy about the fact that they source cider apples from Europe and use juice concentrate rather than fresh-pressed juice. This mix of loyalty to the flavors of regional cider apples grown abroad with the necessary allowances large volume production dictates allows them to, in theory, reduce their carbon footprint while also leaning toward a more hands-on production process, resulting in a more predictably consistent and commercially available product.

As more cideries open across the United States, it's likely some of them will echo this approach. Nurturing new orchards to fruition can take decades, and our current domestic supply of apples may not be able to support a spike in demand. Balancing cost, sustainability, volume, and quality are all trade-offs artisans have to balance for themselves. But it's about the journey, not the destination, and Texas Brut is just as good a place to start as any.

Food Pairings

Austin Eastciders recommends trying Texas Brut with Manchego cheese, a buttery, semi-hard Spanish cheese made from the milk of Manchega sheep. This dry cider bumps up the cheese's distinctive and moderate flavor, and it also goes beautifully with smoked fish or as a Champagne alternative in mimosas. Of course, as a cider that hails from Texas, pairing it with regional barbecue is another great way to keep it local and delicious.

Lassen Traditional Cider //
Newtown Pippin
Chico, California | 8.2%

Many craft beers use sledgehammers to announce their arrival, while balanced ciders tend to rely more on a soft paintbrush. When subtle aromas invite you to come back again and again, each time offering new olfactory sensations, it's a safe bet the beverage you're about to consume will be elegant, complex, and enjoyable.

Lassen's **Newtown Pippin** single varietal dry cider is all of those things. This wild and barrel-fermented cider starts drawing drinkers in with a mild, but fresh scent that one friend of mine described as "cheerful." That friend, Gene Fielden, manages Bottlecraft North Park (one of San Diego's best bottle shops) and is loaded with beer and cider knowledge. Tasting this particular cider reminded him of a Blonde Ale: a smooth, uncomplicated, and approachable American beer style beloved by beginners and advanced drinkers alike.

Thanks to Lassen's relatively hands-off approach to cider making—their ciders tend to be naturally fermented, unpasteurized, and unfiltered—consumers shouldn't expect absolute consistency batch to batch or year to year. But discovering similarities while also appreciating differences is one of the best parts of drinking cider.

About Lassen Traditional Cider

Lassen founder Ben Nielsen began his cider journey much the same way I did—by starting with beer. The homebrewing hobbyist eventually shifted his interest into seeking out the most interesting apples he could find in his own neighborhood until there were no more to uncover, spurring him to adjust his fermentation focus to making cider professionally.

That seems to be where his intersection between the two beverages ends. The further you dive into the Lassen portfolio of ciders, the harder it is to find a bridge between beer and cider. That's a good thing. That same attention to detail and craft remains a common thread between artisan fermenters of all beverages. For Lassen, Newtown Pippin is just the start.

Reverend Nat's Hard Cider //
Tepache Radler

Portland, Oregon | 4.4%

 Nat West, or "Reverend Nat," is a polarizing figure in cider circles. Lauded as either a madman or genius, his unabashed experimentation blurs the lines between every beverage segment in existence, but none more so than the one between beer and cider. Calling himself a cider evangelist who makes "the most unusual ciders that no one else will make," his portfolio of products ranges from the absurd to the ethereal, but outside of apples, it's an obsession with tepache[13] that seems to drive him.

Originally, Radlers were two parts lager to one part fruit juice, typically lemonade, lemon-lime soda, or fizzy grapefruit juice. These low alcohol mixes were concocted to provide refreshment without a quick buzz. In true Reverend fashion, he turns the concept on its head with his **Tepache Radler**, which blends spiced and fermented pineapple juice with dry apple cider for an astonishingly fruit-forward elixir exploding with tropical flavors, candied aromatics, and a medium mouthfeel. With strong notes of brown sugar and rich pineapple, it's hard to define what exactly this is, other than delicious. This one is cider for the beer lovers and the experimentally inclined.

---

13   An alcoholic drink made from fermented pineapple peels, rinds, and juice, which is sometimes back-sweetened with either piloncillo or brown sugar, often with cinnamon added.

West also makes a straightforward 3.2 percent tepache from Costa Rican pineapples, piloncillo[14], and an assortment of spices. Partial fermentation leaves plenty of pineapple-y sweetness, and he suggests mixing this with equal parts Light Lager (something like Modelo or another Mexican lager would be appropriate) to make...a Shandy? A Radler? A lighter Snakebite? It's not cider and it's not beer. Don't think too hard about it and just enjoy.

---

14   Raw Mexican cane sugar whose flavor resembles the deep caramelized sweetness of molasses with a lightly smoky note.

Hoppy Ciders

02

Alternatives to Pale Ales, India Pale Ales, Double IPAs,
and Other Hop-Forward Beers

I love Citra, Mosaic, Cascade, Motueka, and Saaz hops, to name just a few. Knowing that, when I'm faced with choosing between the copious amounts of IPAs on any given shelf or tap list, I'm probably going to go with what I know I prefer. Likewise, I tend to enjoy ciders made with Kingston Black, Yarlington Mill, Hewe's Crab, Porter's Perfection, Dabinett, and Newtown Pippin apples. When I come across ciders containing one or more of these varieties, it's a pretty safe bet I'll end up with an empty glass and a smile.

Cider makers use hops differently than brewers do, adding them purely for aromatic expression and flavor rather than the signature bitterness the beer brewing process extracts through boiling. Beer drinkers who love the bitterness, astringency, aromatics, and flavor of hops in beers like Pale Ales or IPAs won't find an exact replication in hopped ciders. What they *will* find is a new perspective on the individual characteristics of hops when used in a completely different way. "For someone who loves beer and is really unfamiliar with cider, having a common ingredient—being the hops—makes that person more likely to give it a try," says Philadelphia-based Hale & True Cider Company cofounder and cider maker Kerry McKenzie.

It's no accident that the top apple and hop growing region in the United States is the same place: Washington State. Apples and hops both require plenty of water, sunshine, cool nights, and rich soil to thrive, all of which the Pacific Northwest has in spades. They also both have lots of really cool names for different varieties, including Maiden's Blush, Pink Sparkle, Winter Sweet

Paradise, Ambrosia, and King of the Pippins for apples; Fuggle, Apollo, Pacific Jade, Galaxy, and Tomahawk for hops.

Cool names aside, apples and hops can both suffer the same misconception. Those unfamiliar with beer and cider sometimes assume a one-dimensionality of each—thinking hops are just bitter and apples are just apples. But both have hugely wide-ranging personalities, from tropical fruit to cinnamon to pine trees and beyond. Exploring the personality hops can impart to a cider and how they can influence bitterness, flavor, and astringency is sure to excite hop heads and other beer lovers alike.

Western Cider // El Dorado
Missoula, Montana | 6.5%

 Adding hops to cider is a gamble. Cider purists may turn up their noses at what they perceive to be an obvious ploy to entice beer drinkers, and hoppy beer lovers might be daunted by a new use of a beloved staple. But **El Dorado** processes hops a bit differently than many other cideries experimenting with *Humulus lupulus*.[15] Using Montana-grown El Dorado hops, which tend to yield a unique essence of pineapple, lemon, kiwi, and other tropical fruits followed by a lightly resinous scent and flavor, Western Cider steam-distills the harvest into a hop oil, which is blended with the juice of fresh-pressed apples. The result is a deeply aromatic and light-bodied cider with plenty of familiar hop personality, but with little to no bitterness.

Aggressively bitter brews like Double or Triple IPAs don't have similarly belligerent counterparts in cider. That's simply not cider. Instead, hopped ciders like El Dorado keep apples at the forefront, while the hops provide support and balance to symbiotically showcase the finest expressions of terroir from each ingredient.

Food Pairings

When pairing very aromatic, light-bodied beverages with hops in them, I say go big and get spicy. I love a plate of tongue-numbing Sichuan dan dan noodles washed down with a crisp and full-flavored hopped drink. El Dorado's fruit nose and mild pine note on the finish pop brightly when confronted by something scorching, but if the heat's too much, fish and chips or a fish taco heaped with a zesty lime slaw are mild but equally delicious alternatives.

---

15   The genus and species of the common hop.

Ploughman Cider // Lummox
Aspers, Pennsylvania | 6.9%

 Citra hops are a darling of the beer world. (Seriously, who doesn't like Citra hops?) That's one aspect of **Lummox** that makes it an appealing beer-to-cider crossover. Appealing, yes. Unchallenging? Also yes. But boring? Far from it.

Lummox uses a blend of Jonagold and GoldRush apples grown at nearby Three Springs Fruit Farm, a seventh-generation family farm with 200-year-old apple trees. You can't fake that legacy and connection with the earth. Likewise, Citra hops come sourced from Cinderlands Beer Company in Pittsburgh, which occasionally collaborates with Ploughman on even more beer-cider bridges, such as fruited foeder beers. This duo of juicy, sweet, lightly tart, and tangy apples blended seamlessly with Citra hops makes for a smooth cider that leans much more heavily on hop flavor than bitter finish. Together, the trio offers a very green, earthy, dry, and crisp experience familiar to beer and cider drinkers alike.

"Beer drinkers can take what they know about hops and use that as a springboard for exploring apples and terroir," explains Ploughman owner Ben Wenk. Plus, he says, the regionality of Lummox's ingredients provides a peek into the terroir of Pennsylvania itself. "Apples and hops share many famous growing regions of the world, and accordingly, can go great together."

Food Pairings

For Ploughman's first ever cider dinner, the chef paired Lummox with a scallop crudo, which Wenk describes as the perfect nuanced dish to pair with this hopped cider. "I love this cider with seafood," he says, suggesting briny East Coast oysters on the half shell as another option. But of course, he insists, the best pairings are ones yet undiscovered. "Something about the citrus nose of the hops, the subtle fruitiness of the apple blend, and the dry finish makes it very adaptable and food friendly," says Wenk.

The Beer Lover's Guide to Cider

Golden State Cider // Mellow Hops
Sonoma County, California | 6.3%

 Golden State Cider's first iteration of hopped cider was known as Mighty Hops, which was eventually rebranded as Mellow Green before the cidery ultimately settled on **Mellow Hops** in early 2023. A new recipe followed the new name, moving from using intensely earthy Columbus to Cashmere hops in order to include more balanced aromas and flavors of tropical fruit and light herbals.

Part of this evolution is driven by a desire to specifically appeal to habitual beer drinkers, explains Golden State CEO Chris Lacey. "We're using a common, familiar ingredient that people know and love, but they're able to experience it in a different way," he says. "We've had a lot of people try this and really get into cider."

With Champagne yeast, West Coast apples, and plenty of hops, this aromatically driven, dry-finishing cider has plenty of bubbles as well as hop flavor for both beer and cider lovers. Without the typical bitterness found in hop-centric styles like IPAs, drinkers can comprehensively analyze and appreciate every aspect of hops against a bright and sunshine-filled background of fresh apple.

About Golden State Cider

"We have ambitions to become the top selling cider brand in California," says Lacey. It's a tall order, but Golden State has already begun laying their foundation for expansion with its sale to Seismic Brewing Company in 2022. With benefits for both entities like streamlined operations, distribution, and the ability to introduce consumers to both beer and cider at the same time, will we see more partnerships, mergers, and acquisitions between craft beer and cider companies like this in the future? Time will tell, but all signs point to yes.

101 Cider House // Sunlit
Los Angeles, California | 4.5%

 101 Cider House prides itself on focusing more on flavor than on strict category rules. Their portfolio includes ciders with activated charcoal, green tea, yerba mate, and, of course, hops, so it's not exactly the most historically accurate ciderhouse. However, I'd expect nothing less from this splashy, vibrant, wellness-emulating brand from downtown Los Angeles.

Their hopped cider, **Sunlit**, radiates hop aromatics right out of the can, overpowering the accompanying apples and grapefruit peel. That emphasis on hops carries on into the flavor, with the bitterness largely coming from pithy grapefruit rather than hop essence, balancing alongside wildly juicy apple notes that support but don't overshine. With a mostly dry finish and moderately high carbonation throughout, this playful push-and-pull between grapefruit and hops is a dead ringer for a Sour IPA. Still a relative rarity on beer shelves and taprooms, Sour IPAs are one of the more polarizing and boundary-blurring beer styles, but Sunlit gives both hops heads and sour beer lovers something to latch on to with this sessionable hybrid(ish) beverage.

Notes on "Better for You"

Part of me hesitates whenever an alcohol brand espouses a "better for you" ethos. There's certainly an argument to be made that drinking a low alcohol, gluten-free, vegan cider with zero sugar is "better" than chugging a boozy milkshake doused in hot fudge, for example. But there's a fine line between that train of thought and consumers assuming "better for you" means it's literally better for your body, that drinking said product will make you healthier or happier. That's simply not the case, especially when it comes to alcohol.

If you choose to drink alcohol, regardless of sugar content, carbohydrates, calories, or any other measurable nutritional information, remember that "better for you" simply means you have the power to decide what feels better *to you*. Drink with awareness, drink with enjoyment, but above all, drink responsibly.

Peak Light Cider //
Orchard Reserve Quince Cider
Sauvie Island, Oregon | 6.0%

 Ancient scholars referred to quince as "the golden apple," thanks to its rich sweetness, handsome appearance, hardy growth, and its heat resistance, which allows it to flourish in regions typically inhospitable to apples. Quince flesh tends to be too hard to eat raw, but its tart astringency mellows out when cooked, resulting in a fruity, floral, sweet flavor prized in jams and baked goods.

Peak Light Cider's **Orchard Reserve Quince Cider** uses quince's astringency as an advantage. By blending them with late maturing apples, the result is a rich and complex cider that emulates a balanced but crisp and bitter beer, such as a Pale Ale.

No hops were harmed for this cider—in fact, none were used at all. But consumers attuned to the delicacy of craft drinks, regardless of category, are likely to recognize, appreciate, and celebrate the similar ways various beverages can express exciting traits on our palates through different means. In this case, fruit left largely in charge of its own destiny decided to become a pleasantly astringent, moderately carbonated, extremely aromatic, and lightly floral drink. No one will mistake this for a Pale Ale. But if you sit with this, there's a very good chance you'll gain a deeper understanding of the divine sweetness of bitterness.

Food Pairings

Drink this with a small group of friends at sunset, preferably in a quiet, wooded area overlooking a tranquil lake in late summer, ideally with a few fireflies flitting about. Take a sip, then reach for the charcuterie board to select a morsel of smoked summer sausage, a ripe blackberry, and a smudge of soft chèvre. Sit back, let go, and savor.

Eden Specialty Ciders // Treebeard
Newport, Vermont | 6.2%

 It's nice knowing what you're drinking, and Eden does an admirable job of telling you not just what apple varieties are used, but tasting notes and production method information as well, offering a clear picture of exactly what they made and how it came to be. Their fresh hopped harvest cider **Treebeard** also details the types of hops used, which sets them apart via another relative rarity: using a multitude of different hops rather than a single variety.

In Treebeard's case, Centennial, Willamette, and Cascade hops unite alongside a mix of bittersweet and sharp apples (Harry Masters Jersey, Dabinett, McIntosh, and Empire) to emit "notes of pine, citrus, and stone fruit." That sounds a lot like beer to me, but this hopped cider remains one of the more apple-driven ciders both in terms of aromatics and flavor. Its piney, pithy taste and very dry finish sets it up as cider's answer to old school Pale Ales, albeit with the stone fruit dominating flavor rather than supportive malt notes. Even after twenty months in stainless steel, Treebeard's freshness and terroir shines brightly. This one's for hop *and* cider lovers. Availability comes and goes, so if you can find it, get it.

About Eden Specialty Ciders

Eden's transparent approach to cider education extends to their website as well. Clear explanations, concise diagrams, and links to partners and additional resources make learning about cider an easy task. Despite their claim that they come from "a wine point of view," beer experts and beginners alike should rest assured their palates are just as primed to enjoy the fruits of Eden's labor as the palate of any oenophile.

Vander Mill // Hopped Zero
Grand Rapids, Michigan | 6.5%

 Launched in 2006, Vander Mill describes its approach to cider as making products that "straddle the line between traditional and modern." Considering their portfolio ranges from a session cider to cysers,[16] heritage blends, the occasional perry,[17] and beyond, all of these approaches, old and new, still come together under a shared determination to showcase the best of Michigan fruit.

As part of their Zero Added Sugar line, **Hopped Zero** is a bone-dry, wet hopped apple cider that's unfiltered and hazy, but don't call it a Hazy IPA. Wet or fresh hop beers tend to give off strong aromatics and low bitterness, and this cider captures both of these elements, falling closer to a strongly aromatic, very dry West Coast IPA. With a crisp finish, light body, and a somewhat herbal, citrusy, earthy flavor, Michigan hops and apples work together to create a bright and refreshing take on hopped cider (that happens to pair wonderfully with Nashville hot chicken).

About Vander Mill

Vander Mill may embrace traditional techniques, but their ciders can definitely push boundaries. Adding ingredients like spicy peppers, serving ciders on nitro, and collaborating with breweries may seem controversial to a cider purist, but I say why not see how far you can go? Why not be a part of American cider's inevitable redefinition of itself? Classic ciders and techniques have served well for thousands of years. When makers of Vander Mill's caliber and character give experimentation a shot, the results won't please everyone, but at the very least they might open some hearts and minds to the possibilities that come from breaking the rules.

---

16   Mead-cider hybrids made by fermenting honey with apple juice.

17   An alcoholic drink made from the fermented juice of pears.

Hale & True Cider Company //
Hail to the Hop
Philadelphia, Pennsylvania | 6.5%

 Urban cider makers are driving huge potential for the future of American cider. Convenience has become king, and there are only so many rambling country roads drinkers are willing to drive down (and return safely back from) in the hopes of finding great cider. Taprooms and bottle shops located in populated areas allow curious consumers easy access *and* increased choice with less effort.

Hale & True is perfectly poised to preserve their access to fresh Pennsylvania apple juice while appealing to ombibulous urban dwellers by plunking their cidery/taproom in the heart of Philly. "Having an urban cidery brings cider closer to where more people live," says cofounder and cider maker Kerry McKenzie. Convenience aside, McKenzie says having a brick-and-mortar location also gives them an opportunity to provide much-needed, hands-on consumer education about their ciders, including **Hail to the Hop**. "Hail to the Hop definitely acts as a gateway to cider for beer drinkers," he promises.

This cider radiates with Yakima Valley-grown Citra hop aromatics alongside a pithy grapefruit undertone. However, he warns, since the hops are added post-fermentation as part of the dry hopping process, don't expect the same bitterness as in beer. What you should expect is a balanced, refreshing, dry, and crisp drink that just might convince you to reach for this hopped cider rather than an IPA the next time you need a Citra fix.

McKenzie recommends a plate of fresh pasta with cream sauce and mushrooms as a great place to start pairing. "Hail has enough acidity to cut through a creamy sauce, and the floral-grapefruit notes pair really nicely with the earthiness of mushrooms," he says. I'll add truffle and Parmesan fries to the mix of suggestions, as well as smoky dry rub chicken wings or birria tacos to bring out the bright fruit notes.

Fenceline Cider // Catkin
Mancos, Colorado | 6.9%

 Fenceline calls **Catkin** "a cider for the hop lovers," immediately inviting drinkers on a journey to explore Hallertau Blanc and Hüll Melon hops, both dry-hopped with Colorado-grown heritage apples. The pale yellow, slightly fizzy cider emits fresh floral and herbal aromatics suggestive of apple blossoms covered in a light dusting of pollen, followed by bright yet light citrus notes beneath.

Catkin's bitterness remains inconspicuous, leaning toward grapefruit acidity than hop personality, while the German hops express themselves more as a means to achieve complexity than to challenge one's palate. The barest suggestion of sourness comes through as it warms, evolving into green apple, strawberries, and melon, all culminating in a very lightly tart, light-bodied, mostly dry-finishing cider perfect for sipping under sunny skies. The best pairing for Catkin isn't food—rather, it's binoculars, in order to catch a glimpse of one of the many varieties of birds immortalized on Fenceline's collection of cans.

About Fenceline Cider

Situated alongside the Mancos River in southwest Colorado, Fenceline's commitment to upcycling wild apples from abandoned orchards means their products are often one-of-a-kind, inconstant from one batch to the next. But a shared soul connects each one of these ciders not only with one another, but with the earth from which they came, each displaying an irrevocable pledge to craftsmanship and quality. They are all best drunk fresh, preferably at their riverside taproom, but interested consumers outside the area can order online for delivery to (almost) any state.

Colorado Cider Company // Grasshop-Ah
Denver, Colorado | 6.5%

 If we look back at the history of cider making in the United States, hopped ciders are a relatively new invention. Wandering Aengus Ciderworks in Salem, Oregon, is widely considered to have created the first commercially available dry-hopped cider line in the United States under the name Anthem Cider, but producers both large and small have followed suit with their own hoppy iterations.

Established in 2011, Colorado Cider Company was one such early adopter. Their location in Denver, Colorado, one of the country's top beer cities, makes it an ideal place to work on bridging the gap for beer lovers working their way into the cider world. Originally released that same year, **Grasshop-Ah** packs a big citrus punch with huge lemongrass on the nose and tongue, followed by crisp support coming straight from the late dry hop addition of Crystal and Amarillo. Its citrus kick almost completely eclipses hop bitterness, but this medium-bodied, gluten-free, super juicy cider stands to appeal to Hazy IPA lovers or anyone who prefers fruit-forward Pale Ales with flavorful finishes.

Food Pairings

Grasshop-Ah's lemongrass backbone pops when paired with certain Southeast Asian cuisines, such as spicy Vietnamese lemongrass chicken (which can be easily prepared gluten-free) or a vegetarian curry with lemongrass, tofu, and mixed vegetables. I also recommend grabbing a Grasshop-Ah to drink alongside a bánh mì[18] or lumpia[19] for an easy and delicious meal or snack.

Brad Page from Colorado Cider Company suggests pairing this particular cider with charcuterie or cheese, ideally something particularly fatty to complement the cider's crispness. Grab some dry-cured salami, Capocollo, and a mix of semi-soft to firm cheeses like Gouda, Gruyère, or aged cheddar and you've got the makings of an epic pairing.

---

18   A Vietnamese baguette, eaten by itself or as a sandwich.

19   Filipino fried spring rolls.

Wild, Tart & Sour Ciders

03

Alternatives to Goses, Berliner Weisses, Lambics, Gueuzes, and Other Funky, Acid-Forward Beers

Wild, tart, and sour aren't interchangeable concepts. Rather, they encapsulate a large swath of flavors, finishes, and mouthfeels tied more to nature's hand than mankind's. A brewer or cider maker may strategically inoculate their creation with a wild yeast in the hopes of achieving a certain style of finished product, and with experience, they often can succeed. But the unpredictability of this approach to fermentation can attract certain drinkers as much as it repels others.

Beers of this nature can be an acquired taste, and ciders falling within these realms are no different. Ranging from rough and ever-changing to polished and elaborate, wild, tart, and sour ciders provide a captivating way to appreciate similar sensations in a new-to-you beverage. I'd argue it's not only one of the easiest routes from beer to cider, but also one of the most obvious. Sour beer lovers already know—and enjoy—lactic, citric, acetic, and malic acids. Cider just takes it into another dimension.

Sour cider and beer are both really, really old. Sour beer predates pasteurization: a natural byproduct of free-flying yeasts settling on fermenting liquid, giving off a sense of terroir matched by—you guessed it—cider. Cider isn't always sour, but it casts that same impression of time, place, inconsistency, and complexity idolized by sour lovers. Plus, certain wild yeasts and bacteria are known for acidic qualities, which all apple varieties have in varying levels (with bittersharp and sharp containing the highest acid content), so if you *do* like sour beer, you already have a head start on loving cider.

Acid-forward drinks can easily be enjoyed by themselves, but when paired with food, they can transform into something completely different. Spanish ciders from the northern Basque country and Asturias region are arguably the most famous spontaneously fermented beverages in the world, with Spanish "cider throwers," or *escanciadors*, putting on one of the greatest culinary shows on earth. Reaching as high as they can, these skilled servers use one hand to pour an inch or so of cider out at a time to hit the rim of a small glass, held as low as they can in their other hand, in order to invigorate the cider's carbonation, which only lasts momentarily. One gulp and you're done—at least, until the next glass is poured. (If you try this at home, I strongly recommend practicing either outside or over a sink, or at least have a towel handy.) These small sips are often paired with *pintxos*, or small plates.

Spanish cider culture is inextricably tied to food, and the two go astonishingly well together. I encourage you to explore the ciders in this chapter by themselves, but also with food if at all possible. When planning pairings, remember there's a reason cheese, oysters, mussels, dried meats, and other historically traditional Eurocentric pairings have lasted so long—they're great! But our domestic array of Filipino, Mexican, Ethiopian, Cambodian, Korean, and other global options give American cider drinkers a golden opportunity to take food pairing even further.

For those who love tart and bubbly Kettle Sours, refreshing Gueuzes, deeply sour and funky Lambics, or mixed fermentation American Sour Beers and Wild Ales—this chapter is for you.

The Beer Lover's Guide to Cider

Virtue Cider // Kriek (2021)
Fennville, Michigan | 6.9%

 It's impossible to talk about similarities between beer and cider without mentioning Greg Hall. The Virtue Cider founder spent 20 years at the helm of one of the United States' largest breweries: Goose Island Beer Company in Chicago, Illinois, so it's no surprise his beer sensibility and experience has influenced his approach to cider making. Today, many Virtue ciders take cues directly from classic beer styles, most significantly **Kriek**.

Krieks are Belgian Lambic-style beers historically made with sour cherries. The word *kriek* means "cherry" in Flemish, a Dutch dialect used in some parts of Belgium. If you drank this cider blindfolded, you might not realize it wasn't a traditional Kriek beer. It absolutely explodes with aromas of cherry pit, vanilla, and almond—not dissimilar to amaretto, the sweet and bitter almond liqueur. French oak barrels give it just a hint of barrel quality at the finish, and like many Krieks, I find this gets smoother and more complex over time. Since Virtue's come in vintages, expect slight differences in alcohol and structure year to year. However, the heart and soul of this cider will remain the same: strong sour cherry, rich complexity and mouthfeel, and oaky tannins that transport the drinker straight to Europe.

Food Pairings

When in doubt, start with cheese. Soft, pungent cheeses like Brie or a hard, sharp cheese like an aged Vermont cheddar pair wonderfully with this equally intense cider. If you prefer to cut through a rich or heavy dish such as a winter roast or steak, Kriek's cherry sourness and lingering sweetness works nicely here as well. Of course, the easiest option of all remains enjoying Kriek as an after-dinner treat all on its own.

Stem Ciders // A Salted Cucumber
Lafayette and Denver, Colorado | 6.4%

 It can take time to acquire a taste for sour beverages. But before diving into more complicated or complex styles, Goses can act as an approachable entry point into the world of tart or sour beers and ciders. Goses are characterized by high carbonation, noticeable but delicate tartness, light saltiness, and a dry finish. Stem Ciders' **A Salted Cucumber** is a shoo-in for a typical Gose, with a fruit-forwardness that's light-bodied and easy to drink with a marked acidity.

Stem uses 100 percent fresh-pressed apples from the Pacific Northwest, then brings in Cascade and Citra hops during a dry hop addition and finishes with a dash of sea salt and fresh cucumber juice. Even if you're not a huge sour beer or sour cider fan, this is approachable enough to quench your thirst, but unique enough to make one want to try another. What more could a curious consumer ask for?

About Stem Ciders

In 2022, Stem Ciders acquired the Howdy Beer brand and opened Howdy Bar, the flagship taproom for Howdy's Western Pilsner. By offering both beer and cider via different brands, Stem managed to sidestep current regulations that make it difficult (and costly) for a single maker to both brew beer and make cider. Since cider technically falls under wine, companies need separate licenses to make both. But as more makers feel the pressure to produce multiple products, I hope local and national government entities see success stories like Stem and begin to realize how regulatory red tape stifles innovation.

Son of Man // Basajaun
Columbia River Gorge, Oregon | 6.0%

 Son of Man's ciders are made of "nothing but apples and time." This simplistic approach yields enormously complex results across their entire line of Basque-inspired ciders, made in Oregon's scenic Columbia River Gorge. Sagardoa, or Basque ciders, are spontaneously fermented ciders with a highly acidic bite, deeply funky flavor, and a very dry finish more akin to kombucha than beer. Due to the minimal intervention process, apple quality, freshness, and blend of varieties are paramount for creating an exceptional product, like **Basajaun**.

While made in Basque country as part of a collaboration between Son of Man and cider makers Maite Ojanguren and Haritz Urrestarazu, Basajaun remains, at its core, an American take on the wild style. American beverage makers have long danced between paying homage to traditional European styles and channeling that inspiration to a new world audience. Basajaun acts as such a bridge between both, leaving lucky tongues salivating in ecstasy. Funk occupies the centerpiece of this cider altar, so give in to a transcendent experience and try your hand at the ceremonial "catch" of Basque cider to rouse the carbonation and unfiltered yeast. Txotx![20]

Food Pairings & Additional Recommendation

Sour beverages remain the gold standard for bringing out the best flavors of food, and Spanish food-and-drink tradition is the crème de la crème of regional excellence. Basajaun goes best with Basque cuisine, namely grilled seafood and chicken, steak, sardines on toast, lamb and tomato stew, or soft sheep's cheese. If you find Basajaun is a bit adventurous for your taste, try starting with Son of Man's flagship **Sagardo**. It still contains all the fun and funk of a true Basque cider, but its comparatively more delicate flavor and mouthfeel make it an approachable alternative when getting started.

---

20   Txotx, pronounced "choach," translates from Basque to "stick." When shouted in Basque cider houses, it is an invitation, indicating a new barrel of cider has been opened by removing the seal (often a piece of wood, thus the "stick" reference). Grab a glass and get in line!

Dwinell Country Ales // Robin
Goldendale, Washington | 6.3%

 There's something about drinking out of a can that makes even the most exquisite beverage a bit more easygoing. That's especially true in the case of **Robin**, a low acid, pét-nat pear cider made with a blend of Champagne Reinette apples and Packham, Comice, and Taylor's Gold pears. While the 2020 and 2021 vintages use identical fruit blends, only the 2021 harvest blend comes in a 16-ounce can, giving it a familiar feel for beer drinkers who prefer cans over the comparatively ceremonial-feeling large bottles.

On first crack, Robin's effervescence quickly calms, giving off whiffs of mild minerality, fresh pear, and springtime apple ripeness on the nose. If poured into a glass, the lightly hazy, pale yellow liquid almost glows from within, reminiscent more of a luminous sunrise than a flashing sunset. Eventually, Robin culminates with a semidry finish with moderate funk balanced against lingering, clean, pleasant pear at the foreground and apple close behind. A note of salinity delicately prods the residual fruit sugars forward on the tongue, leaving behind a balanced, soft memory of the land that shaped this lucky fruit.

Food Pairings

This mild-mannered cider tastes strongly of the earth from which it came, so I recommend looking toward the sea to complete the experience. Raw Pacific oysters, *moules frites* made with white wine or beer, crab cakes, grilled swordfish, or even a dollop of caviar could all shine if paired here. For a more explosive culinary punch, consider something along the lines of *camarones a la diabla*, a Mexican shrimp dish packed with smoky, spicy flavors ripe for Robin to cut through.

Liberty Ciderworks // Garratza
Spokane, Washington | 7.5%

 Employing time-honored cider making traditions and using locally grown fruit, Washington's Liberty Ciderworks promotes an "inspired by there, but made like here" ethos. **Garratza**, Liberty's take on Spanish *sidra*,[21] uses Dolgo crabapples known for sharp acidity and moderate tannins to create a pungently aromatic cider that draws drinkers in from the first decadent sniff.

Like many Spanish and Basque-inspired ciders, don't be afraid to pour Garratza robustly into a glass in order to rouse the otherwise sleepy cider awake. (Splashing a bit is forgiven, if not encouraged for theatricality.) One sip and your mouth will immediately recognize the wild fermentation of a fairly hands-off product shaped more by nature than by man. Native bacteria give this a moderate mouthfeel that's neither crisp nor cloying, but its inherent funkiness keeps your tastebuds guessing from moment to moment—not unlike Gueuzes or Lambics. While it's unquestionably sour, Garratza remains a manageable walk toward the wild side.

Food Pairings

Liberty owner and cider maker Rick Hastings promises Garratza can be a great gateway for beer lovers familiar with Sour Ales and Goses, calling it "funky, refreshing, and very food friendly." He recommends pairing Garratza with "Basque favorites like flank steak or *Bacalao*,[22] sheep cheese, and olives." I can also see this working with tinned fish, Thai green curry, or *tom yum goong*[23] for equally sharp, but contrasting flavors combining to create a sensational sensory experience.

---

21 Spanish for "cider."
22 Dried and salted codfish.
23 Spicy, hot, and sour shrimp soup.

Durham Cider + Wine Co. //
Life Is But a Dream (2019)
San Luis Obispo, California | 8.31%

Meep Mop, Blump Bloomp Blimp, Everything is Mood, Space Parade—Durham Cider + Wine Co. makes anything but strait-laced or straightforward ciders, starting with their very names. **Life is But a Dream**'s weirdly specific ABV is just another example of Durham's charming idiosyncrasies, with pommelier and namesake Rob Durham describing cider as a "beautiful beverage" that should be "allowed to speak and then gently guided toward balance without manipulation." This type of cosmic harmony is rarely achieved through conventional means, and it certainly seems as though Durham is doing his best to avoid any accusation of convention.

Indeed, this cider keeps organic Gala, Fuji, and Newtown Pippins apples at its core, but—you guessed it—throws expectations out the window by resting the cider for 33 days (no more, no less) on loquats and apricots to create a mouth-puckeringly funky, medium-bodied, spontaneously fermented fruit juice experience that comes complete with its own recommended Spotify playlist. The only commonality I perceive Life Is But a Dream shares with other wild, tart, and sour ciders is that familiar note of light salinity acting as a shot to round out an otherwise flagrant fruit brightness, giving it a depth and complexity that is sure to keep you coming back to see what's changed, even sip to sip.

About Durham Cider + Wine Co.

Are Durham's ciders the most classic ciders you'll ever try? Definitely not. Are they irreverently fun and delicious? Without question. Will different vintages taste the same? Nope, says Durham. "The kind of manipulation needed to produce a consistency year after year takes away from the soul of the beverage," he says, preferring the whims of nature over predictability. "The fruit becomes our guide as we observe and listen to facilitate a journey toward becoming an honest and balanced beverage. The goal is to dissolve the conscious mind, allowing intuition to then take over."

UrbanTree Cidery // Sidra Urbano
Atlanta, Georgia | 7.5%

 Atlanta's first cidery uses Southern-grown apples, which tend to be hardy varieties out of necessity due to their ability to survive hotter summers and warmer winters than more Northern orchards. As climate change's trajectory currently stands, warming trends continue to threaten the very existence of orchards located in said higher hardiness zones, but UrbanTree's commitment to utilizing Georgia-grown apples in its products, including **Sidra Urbano**, continues a legacy of orchardists going back generations. That inimitable taste of time, place, and tradition shines particularly brightly in this Spanish-style cider.

Sidra Urbano is perfect for anyone who wants to dip their toes into funk, but not dive in headfirst. Its restrained tartness finishes mostly dry, but it retains enough tannic structure and smooth fruit sweetness to give a round and full mouthfeel for a pleasantly crisp and lightly funky experience. Unlike other Spanish and Basque-style ciders, Sidra Urbano isn't a test for your taste buds. Rather, it's an approachable option for those early on in their flip flop toward funk.

About UrbanTree Cidery

Many of UrbanTree's ciders have won awards—a noticeable number of awards. As someone who has judged both beer and cider competitions, I hear a lot of (necessary) debate about the accessibility, legitimacy, and credibility of contests. To me, merely entering contests signifies a few things. It means they care about recognition and exposure: a wise business decision for anyone working in an industry with somewhat low mainstream visibility. It also demonstrates an ability to achieve consistency, which isn't always a given when it comes to agriculturally driven products. Third, as a relatively experienced beverage judge, I can say with utter certainty that judges take their jobs *very* seriously, and they tend not to bestow marks of distinction to lackluster products. UrbanTree clearly cares about their craft, so those who value craftsmanship should feel confident giving them a try—before it's too late. It may only be a matter of time before Georgia-grown apples become a rarity in American cider.

Two Broads Ciderworks //
Las Reinas Amargas
San Luis Obispo, California | 7.2%

 This one is for the sour *and* fruit lovers out there. **Las Reinas Amargas**, or "The Bitter Queens," is 500 mL of a jammy, juicy, bittersweet blend made from Washington-grown Porter's Perfection, Kingston Black, Harry Masters, Stokes Red, and Dabinett apples. Two Broads readily admits it's "not exactly to style," but it would be less fun if it was.

A few sips in, and I swore I could taste fresh apricots in this. This light yet exceptionally juicy and tart cider gives off notes of apricot jelly and baked apples, all rounded with a soft oaky note at the dry finish. Like a Flanders Red Ale, this intermingling between fruit complexity, expressive tannins, and moderate acid intensity entices drinkers to contemplatively enjoy how it evolves over time.

The two broads themselves, Maggie Przybylski and Morgan Murphy, have created more than a portfolio of complex and cutting-edge ciders made in California's Central Coast. They've also cultivated an inclusive, equitable, progressive space where anyone who has ever felt like an outsider can feel safe and at home. According to Maggie, their burgeoning cider brand could easily have been a brewery instead. I for one am grateful for their detour to the orchard.

Food Pairings

Two Broads recommends starting with Spanish culinary favorites like a creamy and caramelized Basque cheesecake, Spanish-style paella with beef, chicken, or chorizo (using all three is even better), or aged Manchego cheese accompanied with some dried fruits and nuts. If you're still early on in moving from beer to cider, pair this as you would a Flanders Red Ale. A plate of buttery prawns, a bowl of mussels, a slab of grilled cedar plank salmon, or a luscious spreadable triple-cream cheese like Brie are all mouth-watering options to go with this regal selection.

Reverend Nat's Hard Cider //
Sacrilege Sour Cherry
Portland, Oregon | 5.0%

When a beverage label begins with a warning for intrepid ciderists to beware, the only expectation should be the unexpected. Of course, crafting curiosities is Nat West's modus operandi, so it stands to reason that **Sacrilege Sour Cherry** should follow his unconventional approach to making ciders for the beer lover. In Sacrilege's case, inspiration comes from Lambics, which are very sour, funky Belgian brews crafted to emulate the terroir of specific house yeast strains spontaneously fermented into a wild, complex product.

You'll be forgiven if you mistake this for beer at first sniff. A pervasive cherry complexity, ranging from a sharp sourness to a rich sweetness, shines throughout, followed by a familiar funkiness akin to horse blankets and fresh hay. Consistency is anathema to West, so don't expect different vintages—or even sips taken slowly from the same bottle—to be exactly like what existed before. Various iterations have used Lactobacillus,[24] or what he calls "a cider maker's bogeyman," resulting in a drier finish, higher ABV, and exceptionally tongue-buckling sourness, but you can count on the ubiquitous sour cherry funk to carry through each version of this unpredictable flavor excursion. You have been warned.

---

24 A common but quirky genus of bacteria used in sour beer styles such as Lambics and Berliner Weisses, as well as to ferment foods like yogurt, kimchi, and more. Its use can result in pleasant acidic balance, or venture into imbalance or off-flavors through unwanted infection.

The Beer Lover's Guide to Cider

Additional Recommendation

 Reverend Nat's **Saint Citron** feels as at home here as it might in the upcoming Fruit Cider chapter. Using four different types of citrus (grapefruit, Persian limes, kumquat, and melon) makes a strong argument for this 5.2 percent cider to land in the Fruit category, but it's the added sprinkle of sea salt and ginger that firmly place this in the Gose realm. Saint Citron's fragrance begins with spicy ginger, quickly giving way to a strong lime and melon character reminiscent of a margarita with a fresh-squeezed lime and generous salt rim. Using this many fruits risks a muddled flavor, but each one manages to sparkle on its own.

Potter's Craft Cider // Concord & Brett
Charlottesville, Virginia | 9.0%

 Consumers won't mistake **Concord & Brett** for a craft beer. This limited release comes across more as a wine-cider-beer hybrid than a straightforward style of anything. Wild fermented GoldRush apples are refermented in oak barrels atop Concord grapes for 15 months, giving this bottle conditioned, moderately tannic, dry-finishing, very effervescent Brettanomyces[25] cider a decidedly sour Lambic flair. All the fruit is Virginia-grown, and despite an obvious attraction for wine drinkers, there's enough Brett character throughout to attract sour beer fans of all levels as well.

Thanks to their cider maker Andy Hannas, Potter's Craft Cider is the original cidery to convert me from beer drinker to cider drinker. My appreciation for craft remained the same—it just took me nearly a decade to give myself permission to open my mind and heart to a new beverage. Hopefully, it doesn't take you quite so long. Will they be the cidery to convert you?

---

25 A type of wild yeast commonly used in beer to impart "barnyard" characteristics, such as horse blanket, earthiness, spiciness, or funkiness, it naturally exists on the skin of fruits—like apples—and tends to intrigue beer drinkers as much as it irritates wine makers.

About Potter's Craft Cider

Potter's focuses on using very local ingredients as much as possible, and when "local" means it's coming from some of the United States' most historic orchards and varieties, we're all the better for it. They ship to 39 states, but if you can, I strongly recommend making the journey to their tasting room. Once an Episcopalian church, this stone cathedral now invites drinkers to worship at the altar of cider, all while surrounded by a picturesque, pastoral view of the Blue Ridge Mountains. I can't say for sure what happens after we die, but this seems pretty close to my idea of heaven.

Fruit Ciders

04

Alternatives to Beers that Emphasize Fruit Additions Like Citrus, Berries, Stone Fruits, Tropical Fruits, and More

In a budding industry with few definitive descriptions, the category of fruit cider is a rare example where the definition is both simple and widely agreed upon. Fruit cider is cider in which additional fruits are added to the fermented apple base. Add blueberries and you have a blueberry cider, add guava and it's a guava cider, and so on. To traditionalists, the addition of anything other than fermented apple juice disqualifies the beverage as cider. But thanks to increasing consumer demand and experimentalists working to meet that demand, fruit cider may one day become the backbone of the American cider industry.

American culture thrives on the fringe, and cider is no exception. If craft beer is any indication, there's as much room for convention as there is invention. Keeping in mind that current and future cider drinkers are decidedly less interested in strict category delineations and more interested in flavor above all else, the cider makers in this chapter have dedicated their resources into developing progressive ciders for the modern drinker.

By the numbers, it's a smart move. Fruited beers are more popular than ever before, and there's no reason fruit ciders can't enjoy some of that market share. Breweries like Firestone Walker and The Referend are already harnessing the natural yeast found on fruit skins to make their own fruit-forward wild ales, resulting in complex, often stunning beverages that defy categorization. Others like Ballast Point, Hardywood Park Craft Brewery, and Golden Road Brewing play off popular releases with additions like grapefruit, raspberry, or peach. Adding fruit to a base beverage literally defines "low-hanging fruit" and can help persuade skeptics to give a segment a try.

One thing to keep in mind when tasting fruited beverages is "fruity" doesn't automatically equal "sweet." Figuring out how to untangle our perceptions of fruit sweetness from residual sweetness on the finish takes practice. The ciders in this chapter can help with that. Even ciders made with only apples can express different fruit flavors and aromas, such as lychee, pineapple, orange, and more, thanks to malic acid's versatility across distinct apple varieties. Hops are similar in that way, with flavor notes ranging from grassy to floral, tropical, or citrus fruits.

All the ciders listed here contain fruit other than apple, and like every other category, run the gamut of dry to sweet, straightforward or sour, and beyond to showcase the range of fruit expression. There will always be makers who ferment a base sugar and add artificial fruit flavor later. Thanks to a lack of regulations regarding transparency, it's not always easy to figure out who is using what process. But with time and tasting experience, learning to differentiate between the fruit addition processes in cider will only deepen your appreciation, as well as guide your preferences.

The Beer Lover's Guide to Cider

Bauman's Cider // Strawberry Mojito
Gervais, Oregon | 6.7%

 Christine Walter officially started making cider under the name Bauman's Cider in 2016, but her path toward that destiny started over a century before when her family began farming in 1895. Today, Bauman's portfolio consists of four product lines: Year-Round (modern and balanced), Harvest Series (complex and nuanced), Seasonal (unique and fruit-forward), and Limited Release (small batch and experimental).

As part of the Seasonal line, **Strawberry Mojito** moves effortlessly between a modern approach to cider and a deep respect for tradition and estate-grown ingredients. Using a blend of culinary and dessert apples, Strawberry Mojito's rich aromatics are so intense it's as though someone opened a box of fresh strawberries rather than a bottle of cider. The intensity carries into the flavor and mouthfeel, with full-bodied juiciness in every sip. A hint of fresh mint pops right at the finish—subtle enough to make itself known, but restrained enough to balance a bit of pleasant astringency against the semisweet finish. Walter recommends pairing this luscious and lively cider with "spinach salad, crusty bruschetta with ricotta, sliced strawberries and almonds, or even blended into a cocktail."

About Bauman's Cider

American cider's ownership gender demographics stand out as a more equitable split between men and women than many other beverage industry sectors (especially craft beer). But Walter isn't content to sit on her laurels. As a board member for both the ACA and the Cider Institute of North America (CINA), her efforts to advocate on behalf of the industry stand to make the domestic cider scene a more inclusive, welcoming, and well-known space for all.

Paradise Ciders // Killah Dragon
Mililani, O'ahu, Hawai'i | 6.0%

 Splashed across **Killah Dragon**'s can, shades of magenta and hot pink highlight a sleepy-looking dragon, who gazes directly into drinkers' eyes in a somewhat luring way, daring you to dive in. In its talons it grasps a dragon fruit, with the equally eye-catching fuchsia liquid continuing the invitation to drink this cider from Hawaii's first cidery first with your eyes.

Killah Dragon's aromatics aren't quite as intense as the initial aesthetic, but still give off tropical fruit vibes chock full of dragon fruit and raspberry with a light floral note toward the end. A heavy dose of fresh raspberry mixed with mildly sweet dragon fruit winds down into a structured, semidry finish, but the abundance of fruit well overshadows the light tartness. This abundance of fruit characteristics as the signature element, rather than its tart finish, cast the deciding vote to include Killah Dragon here rather than under Wild, Tart & Sour.

Like a lot of fruit purée styles that fall far outside "beer-flavored beer," this isn't even close to a cider-flavored cider. If you prefer the crispness of a Lager or a very dry cider, Killah Dragon won't be for you. But if it's fruit smoothie flavor with a dash of fermentation you seek, this outrageously tropical option comes packed with a taste of aloha and enough apple to allure adventure seekers. Try it with a bowl of spicy ahi poke, preferably on the beach.

Apples in Hawai'i

Hawaii's climate falls far outside general apple growing territory. However, there are a few apple varieties that can survive at higher elevations in warmer, wetter climates with plenty of sun, including Fuji, Dorsett Golden, and Anna. They tend to have thinner, more delicate skins, so if you get the chance to try any of these tropical varieties, do so at peak freshness.

The Beer Lover's Guide to Cider

Far West Cider Co. //
You Guava Be Kidding Me
Richmond, California | 6.3%

 From the retro-minimalist branding that would look right at home on a beer shelf to the playful names and styles of the ciders themselves, Far West Cider Co. is one of those plucky players in American cider remixing old techniques for a new audience. Its fruit-supplying farm in San Joaquin County goes back four generations, providing their apples as well as seasonal additions such as citrus fruits, cherries, and more.

You Guava Be Kidding Me is an ode to guava rather than apple, starting with its gigantic guava nose, gigantic guava flavor, and gigantic guava finish. Fans of Goses, Kettle Sours, and Berliner Weisses will recognize and appreciate the heavy emphasis on rich fruit flavor with a light body, albeit in a cider that finishes semidry without yeast-driven tartness. This cider isn't a replacement but rather an alternative to beer styles that occasionally have fruit added to them, like New England IPAs, Blonde Ales, or Wheat Ales with a fresh slice of orange on the rim of the glass. Its rich, round mouthfeel lacks tannic structure, instead leaning heavily on tropical notes for a lush, juicy experience that Far West recommends pairing with "tiny paper umbrellas and your favorite Hawaiian mixtape."

Notes About Cider Boxes

Cider box subscriptions are a great way for consumers around the country to access numerous producers at the same time or to explore a single maker's portfolio all at once. Far West's CiderBoxes ship quarterly to 38 states and provide a mix of core ciders along with seasonal releases, one-offs, and other specialty items, as well as first dibs for new merchandise, discounts on tasting room tours, and other perks for signing up. Check and see if your new favorite producer offers a subscription service, or look to multi-maker options such as the Northwest Cider Club for a mix of products from a particular region.

Humboldt Cider Company // Cherry
Eureka, California | 6.5%

 Fruited beverages often cross over the line into sour and tart territory, and those that don't often utilize more citrus-forward, tropical, or sweeter fruits such as mango, passion fruit, yuzu, papaya, strawberry, and so on. In cider as well as beer, cherries almost always exist in that deeply sour realm, thanks to the innate sourness of certain cherry varieties as well as a penchant for similarly dark fruit flavors in aged products.

Humboldt's **Cherry** provides a refreshing take on enjoying cherry for cherry's sake, focusing on the sunshiny sweetness of the fruit rather than its intensity of age or sourness. Humboldt co-owner Michelle Cartledge describes this iteration as a well-balanced, more approachable version of their original sour cherry cider that mimicked a traditional Kriek. This semisweet cider blends apple juice with Montmorency and Morello cherries for a pleasantly crisp finish, spotlighting cherry as a fresh, elegant fruit that can thrive under summer sun just as much as cool winter nights. Plus, the lovely deep, clear crimson hue is as easy on the eyes as this cider is on the palate, and pairs well with dark chocolate or smoky barbecue. Cartledge also recommends adding a splash of Cherry to D.I.Y. marinades for a bit of sweet zest.

Using Cherry in Beer & Cider

According to BJCP guidelines, notes of cherry and other stone fruits are commonly found in European Sour Ales like Flanders Red Ales, Fruit Lambics (like Krieks), and Oud Bruins, ranging from 4.0 to 8.0 percent ABV. Under the same guidelines, the more fluid Fruit Beer designation allows for a much wider range of fruit expression and ABV. The most crucial characteristic is that the fruit itself remains the paramount experience rather than sourness or tartness—in short, as long as it's still recognized as beer, just about anything goes. If BJCP cider guidelines listed commercial examples under "Cider with Other Fruit," I believe Humboldt's award-winning Cherry would be a hallmark of the style.

The Beer Lover's Guide to Cider

Capitol Cider House // Strawberry Blonde
Washington, DC | 6.9%

 Golden yellow and pink-hued GoldRush apples, known for their rich and somewhat spicy and sweet flavor with high acid, blend wonderfully with the jammy sweetness of ripe strawberries in **Strawberry Blonde**, a seasonal release celebrating summer's bounty. Rich culinary aromatics reminiscent of baked fruit tart or strawberry shortcake invite deep whiffs, followed by a light-bodied (but heavily fruited), dry-finishing cider with lots of carbonation and moderate tartness. Fans of light, crisp, tart fruited beers such as Berliner Weisses or Goses can feel confident reaching for Strawberry Blonde as a gluten-free alternative.

Capitol Cider House claims to source all of their apples from within 200 miles of Washington, DC, an area which actually casts a pretty wide net, stretching from Pennsylvania to Virginia. It's as local as an urban cidery can get, and bringing the flavors of the orchard into the heart of a metropolis seems like a practical way to have your terroir and convenience too.

Create an Experience Pairing

Sure, Strawberry Blonde goes well with similarly summery food like spinach and watermelon salad, grilled nectarines, or a goat cheese spread atop rosemary crackers. But with a cider this bright and bubbly, why not take the idea of terroir a bit further and create an immersive experience? Pick up some cans in select stores around the DC area (or have them shipped to one of the 42 states). Head straight for your nearest pool, beach, lake, or other available waterfront location, preferably in the height of summer, armed with clean glasses, comfortable seating, and a new novel. Slather on some sunscreen, crack open a can, and enjoy a taste of the country.

Ironbark Ciderworks // Passionista
Claremont, California | 6.9%

 Ironbark makes all their ciders dry, vegan, and gluten-free with no added preservatives in a wide range of flavors to appeal to a variety of curious drinkers. This approach toward accessibility doesn't stop at their products. Ironbark's on-site rules strictly prohibit any forms of sexism, misogyny, unwelcome touching, homophobia, transphobia, ableism, sizeism, ageism, or any other forms of harassment or derogatory behavior, which results in a safe, welcoming, LGBTQ+ and BIPOC-friendly tasting room. It's wonderful how much better things taste when they're made with respect.

Passionista is crafted with a similar level of respect, using fresh-pressed apple juice mixed with passion fruit juice for a lightly tart, very bubbly, dry-finishing fruit cider that comes across more balanced than big and bold. With its distinctive aroma and taste—as well as its varying ABV by batch, sometimes as high as 9.0 ABV—a little passion fruit can go a long way, and Ironbark's deft hand here results in a wonderfully approachable cider best enjoyed as fresh as possible.

Additional Recommendations

 Ciders containing only apples remain a rarity at Ironbark. Additions such as blood orange, Earl Grey tea, hibiscus, ginger, and even glitter add a bit of fun and accessibility to today's cider industry, especially for those new to the beverage. But it's fruit ciders like Passionista where Ironbark really shines, and **Sassy Simpson** and **Lestat** both deserve honorable mentions. Sassy (with black currants) and Lestat (with blood orange and cranberry) are two similarly dry, light, subtle expressions of their additions that remain rich in fruit sweetness without any residual sugars left behind.

Fenceline Cider // Understory
Mancos, Colorado | 6.5%

Understory, noun: the layer of vegetation between the canopy and the ground cover.

The label for **Understory** begins with a definition of itself, binding to the very earth from which it came. But true understanding of this cider comes later, once you imbibe its lusciousness, which begins with an opulent aroma and ends with a velvety, medium-bodied, semisweet finish. Elderberries have been used throughout history by holistic wellness practitioners for their high level of Vitamin C as well as their dark purple color, which can be used as a natural dye. This striking hue comes through brilliantly in Understory, so I recommend pouring it into a glass to fully appreciate its beauty.

Be sure to savor the deep cherry and dark berry notes on the nose, whose richness somewhat deceivingly emulates beverages with a higher alcohol content. While this smells larger than life, its moderate ABV gives consumers all the sumptuous chewiness of a stronger ale without overt sweetness or a "hot" finish. "Understory is perfect for those looking for a well-balanced fruit cider," says head cider maker Tigo Cruz, pointing to the symphonic interplay between the duo of apples and elderberries, each serving to enhance the other. Make the duo a trio by adding your tastebuds to the composition and enjoy the harmony.

Food Pairings

Like many ciders, Cruz believes Understory goes well with just about everything. But he's particularly keen on pairing the berry-forward beverage with a plate of Greek kebabs marinated in plain Greek yogurt, extra virgin olive oil, a splash of red wine vinegar, and plenty of garlic, lemon, and whatever other herbs you have on hand. I'm partial to grilled chicken skewers, but beef, lamb, or pork also work nicely for a fairly simple dinner party dish washed down with this very lightly tart cider.

Ola Brew // Kona Gold
Big Island, Hawaiʻi | 6.0%

 There aren't many breweries in the United States consistently making their own cider—yet. But in the land where pineapples thrive, it makes perfect sense to find a pineapple cider made with 100 percent Hawaiian grown pineapples and Washington-grown apple juice. **Kona Gold**, the flagship cider from Ola Brew on the Big Island of Hawaiʻi, is another expression of the company's commitment to supporting the local agricultural economy as much as possible, with a bona fide taste of the islands in every sunshiny sip.

With 11 grams of sugar, it's on the sweeter side and engorged with ripe pineapple flavor. Likewise, the aromatics mirror tepache or sugary-sweet pineapple upside-down cake. Pineapple is a common aromatic and flavor in certain hops like El Dorado and Citra, but Kona Gold far surpasses them in tropical expression. It's not quite as hazy as one might imagine for so much pineapple, but throw in a splash of rum and you'd have a heck of a cocktail. This one isn't just for beer lovers; it's for pineapple lovers, first and foremost.

About Ola Brew

This employee and community-owned independent brewery spells out local sustainability as their primary value, letting it guide their operations from top to bottom. By investing in island agriculture, their output remains relatively small, so Ola's beers, ciders, seltzers, and hard teas aren't widely distributed beyond the Hawaiian Islands. However, Kona Gold can be found year-round on the Big Island and beyond, giving consumers a taste of the Kona Coast captured in Hawaii's signature ribbed cans.

Right Bee Cider // Clementine
Chicago, Illinois | 6.0%

Right Bee's ciders are a labor of love, literally. Cofounders Charlie Davis and Katie Morgan document their courtship on every can, starting with Davis's attempts to woo Morgan by making her a cider for her birthday. Apparently, it worked, because two years later Right Bee became Chicago's first cidery, located in the historic Schwinn bike building in northwest Chicago. The rooftop now serves as home to a number of beehives as well, providing fresh (and very local) honey added to a number of ciders.

The limited release **Clementine** contains at least one drop of said honey, along with clementine, cinnamon, rosehip, hibiscus, and of course, apples. This semidry cider begins with lovely floral and citrus notes on the nose, supported by a scent of fresh apple blossom and orange zest. "The most common thing I hear at beer fests from beer lovers is that 'cider is too sweet'," explains Morgan. "Our ciders appeal to beer drinkers because everything is on the dry end."

Don't let the light body deceive you—plenty of mouth-fillingly ripe clementine comes through in the flavor, followed by fresh, juicy apple complexity that's frankly a delight to drink. Each ingredient shines in its own way, coalescing in a wonderful articulation of fresh, fun, and unfussy cider.

Food Pairings

One need only look to a wedge of sharp cheddar cheese to round out the light honeyed sweetness of Clementine. "The light acidity of the cider would work well with cheese," agrees Morgan. She points to the light sprinkle of cinnamon as a unique twist to set this particular product apart from other typically cinnamon-heavy food and drinks. "In our Clementine, the cinnamon is smooth, greeting you on the back end of your sip," she promises. "Like a cinnamon hug!"

Flat Rock Cider Company //
WAtermelon TANGerine
Dana, North Carolina | 6.0%

 On the whole, cocktail drinkers tend to embrace watermelon. However, beer drinkers seem to either love or loathe it, and I haven't seen much in between. Considering this antagonistic divisiveness, I commend Flat Rock for even daring to enter the fray with **WAtermelon TANGerine**, a seasonal cider made with locally sourced apples, watermelon, and a touch of tangerine, and a name paying homage to the iconic Staten Island hip-hop supergroup Wu-Tang Clan.

If you're one of the brash flavor chasers who can't get enough juicy watermelon goodness, you are in luck. This thirst-quenching libation kicks things off with candied watermelon sweetness on the nose, which thankfully balances itself out in the flavor. The tangerine's pithy brightness avoids bitterness and bursts with piquant juiciness, resembling a Hazy IPA or even a Witbier that leans more toward orange than banana or clove. In fact, add a slice of orange to the side of your glass and you've got a watermelon-packed alternative to a Belgian Witbier ready to go. It's not for everyone, but if you like lush, fruit-forward beverages designed to rule everything around you, reach for a WAtermelon TANGerine.

Food Pairings

Bring da ruckus with a few cans of WAtermelon TANGerine to pair with spicy foods, which help highlight its heavy citrus flavors. Drizzle a homemade habanero salsa on top of portobello mushroom tacos, try it alongside jerk chicken, or wash down smoky and savory Nigerian jollof rice[26] for a balanced pairing. For something a bit lighter, consider complementing fruit with fruit by tossing a fresh corn and grilled peach salad together, served sprinkled with fresh mint.

---

26 A popular West African dish typically made in one pot with long-grain rice, fresh tomatoes and tomato paste, peppers, onions, curry, thyme, and other seasonings.

Belgian & Farm house Ciders

05

Alternatives to Saisons, Belgian Singles, Dubbels, Tripels, Belgian Dark Strong Ales, Witbiers, and Other Rustic, Yeast-Driven Beers

In Belgian beer, yeast is king. Spicy, fruity esters and phenols characterize Belgian styles rather than malt or hops, and since cider traditionally lacks both malt *and* hops—while still containing esters and phenols—these styles are a convenient bridge between the two beverages. From Witbiers to Bière de Gardes, Grisettes, Saisons, and beyond, these styles have harnessed Belgian beer culture and transported their long and storied tradition across the world, helping generations of craft beer drinkers learn about and love well-attenuated, highly flavorful, yeast-forward brews. With this already established appreciation, Belgian beer fans are an ideal audience to begin drinking cider.

Farmhouse isn't a strict style. Instead, it's a rudimentary descriptor that indicates a beverage is somewhat rustic, very refreshing, and at least moderately carbonated, with a balance between malt and yeast character. Farmhouse beers generally fall under the Belgian category, but not all Belgian beers are considered farmhouse. Belgian beers can be funky (or not), vary in alcohol content, and are as enjoyable for a casual lunch as they are for a formal occasion.

Farmhouse ciders tend to be tied to an ideal embodied by cider makers who grow, press, ferment, and package their wares within a very small geographical range. Often, the orchard and press are on the same farm (thus, the "farmhouse" designation). These unfiltered, unpasteurized ciders typically use native yeast for fermentation and minimal intervention to mature them into true artisan products, but these are not hard-and-fast-requirements in the United States. Their most distinguishing trait is terroir, that inextricable link to the land that cannot be manufactured or even replicated.

These ciders, like the ones in the Wild, Tart & Sour chapter, pair particularly well with food. Since one of the main characteristics of farmhouse styles is their provinciality, simple, well-made foods like freshly baked bread, hard cheeses, homemade yogurt, fruit tarts, grilled fish, nuts, and olives are excellent starting points for putting together a complementary pairing. Anything that goes well with a Saison will also pair nicely with these farmhouse ciders, and for the more ester-driven options, don't be afraid to get a little spicy. Rich fruit flavor and a round mouthfeel helps wash down even the most Scoville-laden dishes.

Saisons are one of the most show-stopping beer styles ever to exist, surprising plenty of palates formerly resistant to trying beer at all. Belgian and farmhouse ciders stand poised to carry on that persuasive reputation, and these selections are at the top of the list.

Potter's Craft Cider // The Haven
Charlottesville, Virginia | 12.0%

Potter's cofounders Dan Potter and Tim Edmond came to cider by way of beer and homebrewing, so it stands to reason their ciders occasionally take inspiration from said realms. One unmistakable tribute to the Belgian Trappist or "Monastic" brewing traditions is **The Haven**, a Belgian Quadrupel-inspired cider filled with familiar notes of candied fig, coriander, and Belgian yeast character, with dark candi syrup mimicking malty richness.[27] It finishes drier than a typical Quad or Dubbel, but it maintains a classic profile Belgian beer lovers can easily recognize and enjoy. Better still, proceeds from The Haven cider directly benefit The Haven day shelter in Charlottesville, a nonprofit community resource and housing provider supporting unhoused people in the area. The Haven also comes in a barrel-aged version, which sits for 11 months in charred oak barrels previously used by a local winemaker to age fortified red wine. If possible, taste the two versions side by side to discover the nuanced similarities between them, as well as to hone your perceptions of each individually.

Food Pairings & Additional Recommendation

For those who seek an equally complex but comparatively more delicate and refreshing farmhouse beverage experience, Potter's also makes a **Farmhouse Saison**. At 8.0 percent ABV, it's on the stronger side compared to typical Saisons, but contains the same fruity, spicy, well-attenuated personality Saison fans know and love. Belgian Abbey yeast grants rustic esters plenty of structure and space to play, and the blend of Rome and York apples gives it a dry finish and wonderfully lively mouthfeel. Pair it with equally homey dishes such as roasted chicken rubbed with rosemary, garlic, thyme, and lemon; a loaf of freshly baked country bread smeared with lightly salted butter; or French onion soup.

---

27 Candi syrup is a type of syrup with a specific profile of sugars that is made from beets or sugar cane and originates in Belgian brewing.

Texas Keeper Cider // Cider Noir (2021)
Manchaca, Texas | 11.1%

Question: What do you get when you mix a homebrewer, winemaker, and fermentation fanatic? Answer: Texas Keeper Cider. Located just south of Austin's city limits, the cidery can ship to 39 states plus Washington, DC. Locals and visitors to the area can visit their indoor/outdoor taproom and nosh on bites from their food menu full of plates specifically designed to pair with their cider, wine, and mead.

Their rotation of seasonal releases changes, but it's their wintertime **Cider Noir** that makes cider seem even cozier than usual. This imperial strength, small batch cider boasts big notes of pecans, Belgian candi sugar, orange peel, oak barrel, and double fermented apples, including Honeycrisp, Granny Smith, Sweetie, Rome Beauty, Northern Spy, Baldwin, Fuji, Rhode Island Greening, and Piñata varieties. While Texas Keeper's approach to different vintages seems to vary year over year (for example, the 2021 vintage eliminated orange peel, and 2022 had a slightly higher alcohol content of 11.3 percent), the barrel-aged and typical Belgian characteristics remain consistent. When Cider Noir shows up in bottles and in the taproom, fans of strong, complex Belgian Dubbels and Tripels can order one (or two) with confidence.

Food Pairings

Rich citrus and oak notes from the cider pop alongside smoky and spicy foods like barbecue (it *does* hail from Texas, after all), bratwurst, or perhaps a whole smoked cauliflower for a vegan option. The dark candi sugar and hint of orange positively sing when paired with roast duck drizzled in orange glaze, but for the sweet tooths out there, even more options abound. Complement the oak and pecan flavors with something simple like candied pecans or fudge, or outrageously decadent taste sensations like hazelnut truffles or a Belgian chocolate torte.

The Beer Lover's Guide to Cider

Left Bank Ciders // Laughing Jim
Catskill, New York | 8.0%

 From ugly apples comes beautiful cider. Left Bank cofounders Tim Graham and Anna Rosencranz knew the bruised and gnarled apples they saw composted week after week at their local farmer's market still had plenty of life in them and began rescuing them to press at home. One thing led to another, and today, Left Bank makes lovely small batch ciders out of a revitalized space sandwiched between the Hudson River and Catskill Creek.

One of these somewhat hard to attain but very easy to love ciders is **Laughing Jim**, Left Bank's take on a Saison. This somewhat hazy, very dry, very effervescent libation doesn't have the same pillowy head as classic Saisons, but virtually every other aspect is spot-on. Aromatically, Laughing Jim has the expected fresh lemon, light spice, and hint of vanilla on the nose, and its flavor evolves into an even more complex mix of lemon and grapefruit for a balanced and rustic finish that can't help but remind one of home. With a glass of this in one hand and a fresh baguette in the other, fans of farmhouse styles will dissolve into bliss.

About Left Bank Ciders

Despite their relatively small size, ever-changing output, and distribution footprint, Graham believes they have the capability to convert beer lovers into cider lovers en masse. To him, part of the appeal of their ciders is the necessity of seeking them out. "We are tiny, and making weird cider!" he says. "The only place I could see comparing it to would be some funky farmhouse brewery in Europe that no one knows and you have to go way out of your way to visit. That's our vibe, for better or worse."

Far West Cider Co. // Nü Dry
Richmond, California | 6.6%

 Farmhouse ciders manage to be both complex and simple. Their artistry is like that of a loaf of fresh bread, measured not in cups or teaspoons, but in instinct and intuition shaped over generations of oral tradition, and in the joy of sharing the fruits of one's labor with friends, family, neighbors, and loved ones.

It's that balance between allowing nature to radiate its own glory and gently guiding it to its full potential that makes **Nü Dry** a success. Putting a contemporary spin on a venerable beverage tradition is always a risky proposition, but this manages to bring a provincial taste to new and veteran cider drinkers alike. The moderate funk on Nü Dry's nose invites you in with structured brightness, and while the flavor dances close to sourness at times, the light mouthfeel and delicate flavors allow the liquid to flow easily without becoming a challenge. Far West calls it "just a smidge fancy," but this can easily be dressed up for an extravagant feast or dressed down for a fireside hang with friends.

Food Pairings

Start with classic Saison or Champagne pairings and swap those beverages out for Nü Dry instead. Oysters are a no-brainer, as are luxurious seafood dishes such as lobster or even a generous dollop of caviar. The earthiness of truffles marvelously matches the California terroir of Far West's apples, and for cheese, I'm partial to smoked Gouda or even a pimento cheese ball here. A snack of mixed nuts, a side of roasted herbed potatoes, or a well-caramelized crème brûlée for dessert...this is a cider particularly well-suited to a wide variety of food pairings. Experiment and enjoy.

Runcible Cider // Crab Nebula
Mosier, Oregon | 7.3%

Crab Nebula has a great name, and it has a great label. Luckily, it's also a great cider. This sparkling farmhouse cider from Runcible Cider is just one of their farmhouse-inspired offerings, described as "hard, but not difficult," where even the intricate becomes explainable.

Made with heritage varieties blended with crab apples, this naturally sparkling and dry-finishing cider is made using traditional methods, resulting in a balanced acid-to-tannin ratio just funky enough to keep things interesting. Since it's unfiltered, there's a bit of yeast settled at the bottom of the resealable bottle, so for best results, pour gently (but sip vigorously) in order to bring out its lively, lemony, lightly hazy farmhouse personality. Crab Nebula is a delightful steppingstone for those who appreciate an arcadian taste of place expressed through the hand-picked apples of the Columbia River Gorge.

About Runcible Cider

Runcible itself is a nonsense word, first coined by Edward Lear and famously used in his 1870 poem *The Owl and the Pussycat*. Many cultural references have been made using the term since then, from song lyrics to science fiction characters. The cidery adopted the term in homage to their whimsical and spontaneous approach to cider making—an apt concept from which to draw inspiration. In true cider tradition, the cidery doesn't seem to be particularly inclined to grow beyond its existing borders, so if it's at all possible, honor their locality by enjoying these farmhouse ciders as close to the farm as possible.

ANXO Cider // Happy Trees
Washington, DC | 6.9%

 Funk, fruit, and farmhouse—ANXO Cider's **Happy Trees** dances across the spectrum of flavors to provide a palate-pleasing cider for a multitude of tastes. 100 percent Virginia-grown Albemarle Pippins left to naturally ferment in casks which previously held Sangiovese[28] gives Happy Trees a luscious depth immediately apparent upon opening. Its scent is instantly wild and unpredictable, ranging from farmhouse funk to wine tannins and earthy apples mixed with just a hint of tropical fruit.

Its intricacies don't end with the scent. From the first taste, this moderately carbonated, dry-finishing cider seems to change with each passing moment, following flexible style boundaries more akin to the natural wine movement than to a process-heavy brewing approach. But it's the spontaneous, wild fermentation character that serves to attract the habitual beer drinker. Styles like Brett Saisons are beloved by some, but bypassed by others in favor of a more conventional iteration of the Belgian beer category. However, these funky farmhouse beverages can capture the imagination of beer aficionados, wine drinkers, and cider fans alike.

---

28   A rustic, dry Italian red wine with high acid and tannin levels.

About ANXO Cider

ANXO is a cider ambassador, appealing not just to drinkers across different categories, but people across different identities, experiences, and backgrounds as well. Their collaborations with English cider makers opened the door for cider culture to hit American shores, while their partnerships with companies like Beer Kulture and the ACA provide opportunities and scholarships for marginalized people to learn about, drink, and enjoy cider. ANXO's Pride cider raises money for the Human Rights Campaign, and they collaborate with women-owned cider companies like Eden Specialty Ciders to fundraise for women's health. The list goes on, but the takeaway remains: Drink ANXO and do good.

Artifact Cider Project // Wolf at the Door

Cambridge and Florence, Massachusetts | 6.0%

 Saisons have inspired a lot of loyalty over the centuries. The super dry, super bubbly farmhouse brew appeals to entry-level drinkers as much as longtime beer experts, and there's just enough flexibility in the style to play around with its rustic characteristics. But **Wolf at the Door** isn't here to play.

Its house mixed yeast culture doesn't smother you aromatically with horse blanket or transport you to a barnyard as some phenolic-forward beverages tend to do, but it definitely hints at what's to come. What *is* to come? A structured, bone-dry cider made with Yarlington Mill and McIntosh apples, packed with acid, a decent quantity of supportive tannins, and a striking similarity to Saisons, albeit slightly less effervescent than a classic take on the style. There may very well be a wolf at the door, but you should take your chances on it.

"Wolf is one of our most versatile ciders for pairing," says Soham Bhatt, cofounder of Artifact. "Anything with fermented funk (any European farmhouse cheese, or fermented Asian condiments like *doubanjiang*[29]) or spice goes wonderfully—it cuts richness with tannin. Best pairing I've ever had with it—maybe for cider ever—was a steam-coming-out-of-your-ears spicy goat *biryani*[30] at Dhamaka in NYC."

---

29 Fermented Chinese bean paste often used in Sichuan cuisine.

30 A classic Indian dish made with long-grain rice, slow-cooked meat, and fragrant spices like cumin, turmeric, garam masala, and more.

A similarly farmhouse-inclined option from Artifact is **Last Light**, a beautifully icy pale and crystal-clear cider bursting with horsey funk aromatics and light minerality. Its mouthfeel is more crisp than chewy, and its light body, low ABV (4.2 percent), and provincial undertones could easily appeal to hard seltzer fans as well as Chardonnay drinkers. I happened to pair this with homemade spicy kimchi and *okonomiyaki*.[31] The low-to-moderate residual sweetness of the cider perfectly accented the meal's umami components, leading to an unexpected but gratifying combination.

---

31 A savory Japanese pancake typically pan-fried and drizzled with Japanese mayonnaise, seaweed or bonito flakes, and a Worcestershire sauce mix.

Graft Cider // Farm Flor
Newburgh, New York | 6.9%

 It's springtime. You're sitting atop a hillside blanketed with daisies and buzzing with busy pollinators, gazing down at a glinting creek sparkling in the late afternoon sun. As the day slowly ebbs toward dusk, an ancient oak tree's shadow cuts across the time-softened and fringed picnic throw. The picnic basket's woven handle mirrors the splintered shutters of the weatherworn barn to your back, long since emptied of livestock and hay bales. Whiffs of seasonal change waft through the air, along with dandelion spores, an errant clover leaf, and a hint of a crackling campfire far off in the distance.

If this pastoral scene had a taste, it would be **Farm Flor**. It's not quite a Saison or a Bière de Garde; it is its own category of rustic cider, with a dry, tart finish and soft flavors from fresh lemon to light oak. Earthiness and effervescence abound across this delicate and complex cider that quenches thirst as much as it invites you to sip again and again.

About Graft Cider

Launched by the brother-and-sister duo Sara and Kyle Sherrer, Graft's mission is to invite cider explorers on a journey of discovery and delight. By taking inspiration from craft breweries, they've managed to position themselves at the forefront of new American cider by meshing traditional cider techniques with flavors quite similar to beer or even cocktails. As they look to the past to create a new future, a fresh generation of cider enthusiasts is ready to be born.

Wild Hare Cider // Bloom
Shenandoah Valley, Virginia | 6.9%

There's no such thing as "girl beer," but Belgian White Ales and Witbiers in particular seem to have a hard time shaking off a sexist reputation as flaccid, fruity drinks. This close-minded misconception really is a shame, because they're some of the most approachable, thirst-quenching, and delightfully complex beer styles out there, with enough mouthfeel heft and complexity to keep things interesting, while remaining light enough to quickly crush on a hot, sunny day.

Wild Hare Cider describes **Bloom** as a gluten-free tribute to these fruited Belgian White Ales, notably those with prominent orange character on the nose and in the flavor. This easy-drinking, highly carbonated cider bursts with Belgian personality, offering more orange pith than juice in mouthfeel and taste. The semidry finish refreshes the tongue, while coriander, orange blossom honey, orange peel, Azacca hops, and heritage apples grown in the Shenandoah Valley all work together to create a bright summer sipper that cider and beer lovers can enjoy. Orange slice optional.

Food Pairings

A fresh salad with tomatoes, cucumbers, carrots, and other summer vegetables lightly tossed with green goddess dressing makes an ideal companion to this bright and juicy cider, as does your favorite sushi dish, citrus-marinated meat or fish, steamed mussels, or simple sandwiches like chicken salad or ham and Swiss. If you're compiling a cheese board to pair with Bloom, be sure to include some buffalo mozzarella, burrata, or another soft, creamy option to balance alongside the orange notes. Add some smoked salmon pâté on herb crackers or a few mild fruits like kiwi and dried apricot, and you have the makings of a true feast.

Mt. Defiance Cidery & Distillery //
Farmhouse Style
Middleburg, Virginia | 7.2%

 Horses, hounds, and hunting are a way of life in this rural Northern Virginia town, so it stands to reason they make excellent farmhouse ciders. Using Virginia apples, **Farmhouse Style** remains well-carbonated and light-bodied throughout, encapsulating the concept of understatement: subtle, yet sophisticated; delicate, yet delicious. It's as straightforward as a farmhouse cider can get (it's in the name, after all), yet seems to transform with time, highlighting the terroir of Old Dominion in simple terms even a novice cider drinker can appreciate.

Besides capturing the soft tartness and pastoral perfection of its surroundings, Mt. Defiance's other strength has to be the breathtakingly picturesque locale of The Cider Barn, located less than a mile down the road from its separate distilling facility and spirits tasting room. Sitting atop a rolling green hill overlooking the splendor of the Blue Ridge Mountains, the wood-paneled indoor/outdoor space has a sprawling wraparound porch and in true Southern fashion, plenty of rocking chairs to slowly sway your troubles away.

Food Pairings

Virginia cider thrives with Virginia food, so anything regional, seasonal, or Southern can dazzle alongside Farmhouse Style. Fresh-baked biscuits smothered in homemade jelly, shrimp and cheesy grits, or even country-fried rabbit with collard greens or roasted root vegetables would all work nicely, as would any gamey meat or earthy veggie, such as morel, porcini mushrooms, or roasted turnips and squash. For something sweeter, this cider's subtleties would sing alongside a silky panna cotta with a sprinkle of cinnamon, or even a dollop of apple butter. Its versatility is its strength, so pop a bottle and see what works for you.

Imperial Ciders

06

Alternatives to Barleywines, Old Ales, Bocks,
Barrel-Aged Beers, and Other High-Alcohol Beers

Hands down, the biggest indicator of consumer purchasing decisions is flavor. People—especially younger Americans—increasingly care less about what a drink *is*. They just want to know what it tastes like. After flavor, factors like price, packaging, variety, freshness, independent ownership status, and scarcity all affect a consumer's ultimate choice, but alcohol content remains another one of the top value points for prospective and new customers.

Perceived value tends to drive Americans' desire for higher ABV drinks (even as low- and no-alcohol options blossom across all segments), and products at or above 8.0 percent ABV, which are considered "imperial," are some of the biggest contributors to cider's growth in the US. This trend has doggedly persisted, even in the face of the confusing and inconsistent regulatory hurdles outlined earlier. Previous to 2020, American ciders over 7.0 percent ABV needed an exemption from states in order to be packaged in 12-ounce cans or bottles. Once the TTB updated national regulations to allow 12-ounce packaging for higher ABV ciders, the imperial category exploded.

When yeast breaks down fermentable sugars, it creates alcohol. In cider, that sugar comes directly from the apples themselves and any other ingredients added to the mix, like other fruits. Depending on how much sugar ferments out of a cider, it can finish anywhere from bone dry to very sweet. Generally, a higher sugar content leads to a higher alcohol content, but this doesn't mean that all high-alcohol beverages taste sweet. The ciders in this chapter include a range of finishes, showcasing the breadth of American ingenuity and skill within a rapidly developing subcategory.

While the vast majority of American craft cider falls outside the imperial realm, this niche might be one of the easiest tracks for beer lovers to take when experimenting with cider. Although malt expression remains absent in cider—meaning counterparts to malt-centric styles like Stouts, Porters, or Brown Ales don't really exist—familiar touchpoints like barrel quality, alcohol warmth, and hefty mouthfeel can make these big craft ciders an attractive alternative to big craft beers.

Two Broads Ciderworks // Frost
San Luis Obispo, California | 16.1%

 Frost is a fresh spin on ice cider, a style originally invented in 1989 by Christian Barthomeuf, 5,000 miles away from San Luis Obispo in Québec, Canada. *Cidre de glace*[32] is typically made via cryoconcentration, a process where makers press apples and freeze the juice in order to separate water from the concentrated sugar, creating a sweeter liquid with a higher alcohol content.[33] Using this process after a long, slow fermentation, Two Broads mellows their juice in French oak barrels for a year, resulting in an utterly rich, chewy, piquant, and full-bodied beverage suited for after-dinner sipping and savoring. If you happen to have a cozy blanket and roaring fire, so much the better.

Beer lovers who appreciate barrel character will find copious amounts to enjoy in Frost, as well as a familiar blend of light vanilla, candied orange, and rich plum found in certain Belgian beer styles like Belgian Dark Strong Ales. With a drier finish and higher alcohol content than what's standard for Québecois ice ciders, Frost manages to balance sweet with heat for a surprisingly sippable strong cider. Don't feel as though you have to finish it in one go—ice ciders can be corked and stashed in the refrigerator for later consumption.

---

32   French for "ice cider"

33   A less commonly used practice, known as cryoextraction, allows fruit to freeze on the trees to similarly reduce the fruit's water content before pressing.

In 2014, the Canadian province formally established Protected Geographical Appellation (PGI) guidelines Québec's ice ciders must meet in order to use the official "PGI Cidre de glace du Québec" designation, including an ABV range between 7.0 percent and 13.0 percent; no use of artificial flavors or colors; and the cider must be pressed, prepared, and bottled at the site of production (plus quite a few other requirements). In 2022, the ACA began efforts to officially adopt the same quality specifications for American-made ice ciders—another step in unifying loose cider concepts under one roof.

Eden Specialty Ciders // Heirloom Blend
Newport, Vermont | 10.0%

 One name rises above the rest when talking about strong cider made in the United States: Eden, the United States' first commercial ice cider maker. Eden's first batch of cider ever was ice cider, or what they call "the soul of the apple in liquid form," and it arguably remains the magnum opus of their impressive portfolio. **Heirloom Blend** uses only locally grown heirloom apples, and a lot of them. They estimate it takes over eight pounds of apples to make one 375 mL bottle, and with a lead time of one to three years to complete, it takes a lot of time, patience, and care to bring this dessert-style cider to fruition.

It's well worth the wait, absolutely bursting with golden honeycomb and baked apple flavors that go down much more easily than most drinks with a double-digit alcohol concentration while still maintaining a long, slow finish. Smooth, silky, still, sweet, and strong, Heirloom Blend sets the standard for American-made ice cider. Fans of strong and sweet beer styles such as Eisbocks can confidently reach for a bottle of Heirloom Blend to experience the same rich complexity and pleasurable warmth from a different perspective.

Food Pairings

This style's inherent sweetness tends to balance well against exceptionally savory or salty dishes, including blue cheese (the more pungent, the better), salt-cured ham, or even popcorn if you're in the mood for munching. Ice ciders are typically served chilled, but as Heirloom Blend warms to room temperature, new intricacies begin to reveal themselves in fresh ways (meaning if you choose to sip this à la carte, you'll still have more than enough dimensions to appreciate in the cider by itself). Ice cider also ages well—*if* there's any left after opening this bottle of liquid light.

Number 12 Cider // Barrel 44
Minneapolis, Minnesota | 10.8%

 Number 12 Cider promises their ciders are full of surprises, and this imperial strength, bourbon-barrel-aged cider is one of them. If **Barrel 44** were beer, it would live along the periphery of Strong British Ales. But rather than straightforwardly replicating any one style within the category, Barrel 44 deftly emulates characteristics from each: the dried fruit and toffee sweetness of an Old Ale; the body, warmth, and ester characteristics of a Wee Heavy; and the low head retention, aromatic intensity, and higher alcohol content of an English Barleywine.

It also incorporates a somewhat more British mouthfeel than many lighter, crisper ciders, relying on a more rounded finish and effervescent body to boost its barrel characteristics. Number 12 avoids unpleasant and volatile heat from the alcohol content, thanks to the luscious caramel, vanilla, and toffee sweetness that blunts any sharp edges. It smoothly slides across the tongue like silk, and Number 12 Cider co-owner Colin Post says to look for flavors like vanilla, smoky bourbon, molasses, and apricot as Barrel 44 evolves with each sip. He recommends letting it warm to around 50 degrees Fahrenheit in order to enhance the complex flavors and aromas that come from its long creation process.

"One of the keys to Barrel 44 is that it is fortified and then refermented in the bourbon barrels, not just still-aged," he explains. "This more rigorous process captures the bourbon and barrel essence and adds layers of flavor that can be difficult to achieve with just apples or simple barrel aging."

Food Pairings

Post recommends pairing decadence with decadence, suggesting a Kobe beef burger topped with aged cheddar, caramelized onions, and crispy bacon. "With its higher ABV and stronger flavor presence, the cider holds its own and balances sublimely with the richness of such a burger, or even a smoky rack of ribs," he says.

Virtue Cider // Flok (2022)
Fennville, Michigan | 12.1%

 From wine glasses to beer mugs and cocktail coupes, many drinks, like Martinis, have their own trademark glassware easily recognizable at a single glance. While cider has yet to embrace an industry-wide signature vessel to drink from, ice cider's tall and skinny bottles act as a visual hint to signal their position alongside many dessert wines.

One benefit ice cider provides as an alternative to traditional dessert wines is cider's inherent inclination toward balance over intensity. While **Flok** clocks in at 12.1 percent, it never burns unpleasantly on the tongue or sticks around with a cloying cling. Instead, its bright and intense aromatics engage the senses, encouraging careful sensory exploration and appreciation from start to finish. The Michigan apples remain at the vanguard, reminding drinkers this *is* cider, after all, followed by copious notes of honey, caramel, butter toffee, and French oak barrels. Flok's dangerously smooth and semisweet finish allows it to stand alone or mixed in a cocktail—a "Floktail," according to Virtue. If experimenting with mixology, I recommend adding a dash of acid to bring out even more brightness, something with citrus or cranberry for a bit of punchiness.

Additional Recommendations

Virtue's extensive beer sensibility and large portfolio of cider options make it hard to pick one or two options for beer lovers. Any ABV chaser won't have to look far here: Their **2021 Mitten** blends range from **Bourbon County Brand Stout Mitten** (10.1 percent) to **Double Barrel Mitten** (12.6 percent) and even a **Triple Barrel Mitten** (13.8 percent). This is an ideal lineup for a side-by-side tasting in order to appreciate the similarities and differences between the three. Do you have enough restraint to collect next year's set for a vertical?

Western Cider // Dry & Dandy
Missoula, Montana | 11.0%

It's said that we drink with our eyes. If that's the case, then Western Cider's **Dry & Dandy** is delicious before it's even (slowly) opened. No, seriously—open it slowly. This pét-nat has a lot of bubbles and they are not afraid to gush!

From the cool label illustration to the gorgeous toffee and light amber hue to the tantalizing flavor itself, Dry & Dandy hits all the high notes with similarities to malt-driven beer styles such as the color, mouthfeel, and toffee sweetness of a Dark Mild or British Brown Ale; the strength of an English Barleywine; and the complexity of certain Bock beers. Starting with luscious and deep aromatics, this cider bubbles over with butterscotch and honey scents, inviting drinkers in without straying into an overly sweet cloy. Tannins and a medium body mimic a malt profile, giving dark and imperial beer lovers a familiar mouthfeel to hold onto while offering something wholly new. Western says this is "eminently drinkable." I'm inclined to agree.

Additional Recommendation

The alcohol content in Western Cider's products tends to fluctuate (Dry & Dandy has been as high as 11.0 percent and as low as 8.1 percent ABV), but their imperial offerings all provide a similarly robust experience with gratifyingly broad tasting notes. **Whiskey Peach** (10.0 percent to 11.0 percent) is one such example, with flavors of dried fruit, vanilla, and apple alongside a woody barrel character and an inviting hint of alcohol warmth. It's deceptively smooth, with balance coming from the white oak whiskey barrels and peaches for an enjoyable sipper with as much charisma as restraint.

Angry Orchard // Wooden Sleeper
Walden, New York | 7.0%

 Considering the second-largest craft beer company in the United States (Boston Beer Company) owns the largest cider brand in the country (Angry Orchard), it makes sense that Angry Orchard brings a beer perception into the cider realm. Their craft edge comes from their small batch cider house offerings like **Wooden Sleeper**, a 16-ounce canned cider blend aged in bourbon barrels for one to two years and only available for sale in New York State.

Despite its delightfully spooky can design, Wooden Sleeper is more scrumptious than scary, with huge whiffs of pumpkin spice, fall leaves, and autumn spices followed by a hearty helping of bittersweet and bittersharp apples and just a hint of bourbon barrel on the nose. Its beautiful clear golden color, medium mouthfeel, and barrel flavor—without too much heat—all serve to entice bourbon barrel beer lovers to consider this as an alternative with a lower alcohol content than many imperial or aged beers. By itself, Wooden Sleeper has all the flavors of fall. Paired with foods like broccoli cheddar soup, meatloaf, or Dutch apple pie, the flavors of fall start to meld into the coziness of winter.

About Angry Orchard

The vast majority of Angry Orchard's offerings are available year-round and across the United States. However, the small batches and one-offs coming out of their Innovation Cider House in Walden, New York prove that even the little guys can play with the big dogs. Despite insistence that cider should not be compared to beer, I bet that anyone with an appreciation for craft—whether it be craft beer or craft cider—can find something to enjoy from their limited release lineup.

Finger Lakes Cider House // Pommeau

Interlaken, New York | 20.0%

 If Napa, California is the capital of American wine, the Finger Lakes region of New York State is the capital of American cider. Not only is it the second-largest apple producing state in the US after Washington State, but its rich orcharding tradition, distinctive glacial soil composition, and microclimate guided by the lakes themselves all create a one-of-a-kind experience from farm to glass.

Although the land's history goes back for generations, Finger Lakes Cider House on Good Life Farm has been at the heart of the region's cider renaissance since opening in 2015. Cider is widely considered to be the quintessential "American beverage," but pommeau is a distinctly French invention that American makers continue to fiddle with to fortuitous results.

This particular **Pommeau** takes that European style and transforms it into something original, blending unaged apple brandy with fresh juice from Golden Russet, Dabinett, and Margil apples. The concoction then ages in American Oak barrels for at least 18 months, resulting in an ambrosial fireside sipper ideally served at room temperature. Strong notes of rich caramel, anise, oak, and dark fruit come off the nose, with a bountiful mouthfeel and honeyed finish containing just enough heat to comfortably slow you down.

Mixing Beer and Pommeau

Although this Pommeau's high alcohol content doesn't really need a boost, one surefire way to tiptoe toward appreciating the style is by mixing it—with beer! Gene Fielden from Bottlecraft let me in on a little secret: If you have a Stout that's just a bit too toasty for your taste, add a few drops of your favorite Pommeau to cut through the malt roastiness and balance it to your liking. If you enjoy the richness of Finger Lakes' Pommeau as-is, pair it with pâté before a meal or alongside your preferred dessert after.

2 Towns Ciderhouse // Cosmic Crisp
Corvallis, Oregon | 8.0%

As one of the biggest cider companies in the United States, 2 Towns has made a national name for itself through consistency of execution and approachability of styles. However, it's in their imperial offerings that 2 Towns defines itself and the cider category at large. At 8.0 percent ABV, **Cosmic Crisp** tiptoes on that line between standard strength and imperial, all while retaining the classic 2 Towns congeniality with balance, bubbles, and bright fruit.

Cosmic Crisp smells hotter than it tastes, with explosive flavors of juicy fresh apple, moderately high structure, and a dry finish to provide a deceptively complex and acid-forward cider that keeps you coming back. Although 2 Towns recommends enjoying this cider chilled, over time it gains an inviting sophistication ideal for mixing with spirits or even using in baking recipes. (Check the 2 Towns website for specific cocktail and cooking suggestions, including a Cosmic Mule and an Apple Fizz.)

Food Pairings & Additional Recommendation

If the number of awards won are any indication, there's something good about **The Bad Apple**. There's no mistaking this bold cider as anything but imperial, but even at 10.5 percent ABV, it retains a smooth balance that's as appealing as it is alluring. Using meadowfoam honey and aged on white oak, The Bad Apple boasts huge notes of vanilla, fresh blossom, and light honey with a balanced finish.

Like Cosmic Crisp and most of 2 Towns' ciders, this is best enjoyed chilled and paired with rich stew, soft cheese, or cured meats. Vegetarian or gluten-free home cooks can also try their hand at 2 Towns' "Bad Apple Tofu Turkey" recipe, which uses a bit of The Bad Apple as an ingredient, but leaves plenty to enjoy during the cooking process.

Schilling Hard Cider // Original Apple
Oregon and Washington State | 8.4%

 Originally launched in Seattle, Washington, in 2013, Schilling Hard Cider now produces more than 100,000 barrels of cider annually. If they were a craft brewery, they would easily fall in the top half of the 50 biggest craft breweries in terms of output. Available across 20 states with taprooms in Seattle, Washington, and Portland, Oregon, it's one of the larger regional breweries in the American West and one of the most ambitious.

Although their imperial line of Excelsior ciders is small—only three canned ciders are currently available—the ciders themselves are anything but. At 8.4 percent, **Original Apple** offers a balanced if not ever so slightly sweet take on the imperial category, with a lovely dark orange hue similar to a Strong Bitter or English IPA. Schilling calls it "crushable," but I'm not sure it's advisable to "crush" anything over 6.0 percent. Still, its drinkability is notable, with a pleasingly light but rich heirloom apple aroma and high acidity that results in an easy-drinking cider with a bit of buzz behind it.

Notes About Imperial Ciders

As one of the driving forces behind regulatory change, CEO and cofounder Colin Schilling plays a large part in imperial cider's growth across the US. "We want to showcase how great cider can be, that not all cider is sweet, and that the craft of cider making has a wide range of possibilities with something for everyone," he explains. After switching to six-packs of cans from 750 mL bottles (the previous standard for cider packaging), consumers can now access higher ABV ciders at a lower price point and in a more familiar format. That ease of accessibility with a wider range of alcohol content, as well as cider's gluten-free nature, make imperial ciders one of American cider's most promising avenues of future growth.

Durham Cider + Wine Co //
These are the K.B.'s (2020)
San Luis Obispo, California | 8.2%

In keeping with Durham Cider's unorthodox operating procedure, **These are the K.B.'s** is a punchy pét-nat using the same apples—in this case, only bittersharp Kingston Blacks—to achieve slightly different results year over year. Single varietal ciders provide a fantastic opportunity to dive into the dimensions of specific apple profiles: acid and tannin levels, sweetness, flavor, aroma, color, body, and so on. There are very few apples that achieve cider's desired balance by themselves, but Kingston Black apples remain one of the few well-suited for a solo.

This single varietal cider is anything but one-dimensional. Its vivacious carbonation gives the lightly hazy, gorgeous gold liquid plenty of opportunity to sparkle in the glass as well as on the tongue. Mild but rich aromatics do more than hint at what's to come—they're an ode to the classic cider apple known for finicky growing habits. But consumers are the ones reaping the rewards here, with huge notes of juicy orange and apple, a moderate astringency similar to beer's bitterness, and a medium mouthfeel that comes across bright and fresh, while also deeply ancient and exploratory.

Food Pairings

These are the K.B.s is as easy to drink as it is crucial to pore over. Thanks to its very high carbonation, orange essence, and tropical fruit notes, this cider could easily find a home at any breakfast or brunch table in lieu of a mimosa or other sparkling fruit cocktail. If, like me, you'd rather fill up on small bites than wait for a main course, slather some goat cheese on crackers or fill a plate with crab cakes or even a few bites of *takoyaki*.[34] This cider's intrinsic fullness holds its own against the epicurean appetizers.

---

34 A Japanese street food snack made of wheat-battered octopus, pickled ginger, and green onion shaped into a ball, then sprinkled with seaweed flakes and drizzled with mayonnaise and takoyaki sauce (similar to okonomiyaki sauce, but often a bit sweeter and thicker).

Specialty Ciders

07

*Alternatives to Rauchbiers, Pumpkin Beers, Specialty
Styles, Seasonal Beers, and Other Esoteric or
Experimental Beer Styles*

Across the United States, certain segments of beverage alcohol with reputations for big, bold flavors are often prized for intensity rather than balance. This is perhaps most pervasive throughout American craft beer—not all craft beers lean toward the extreme, but the ones that do certainly make headlines. Perhaps it's our innate inclination toward the counterculture or our tendency to celebrate innovation over tradition, but American cider has taken up the mantle and begun to push the boundaries of what could reasonably be considered cider in order to lure consumers more interested in flavor than specific category.

Despite cider's overarching tendency to romanticize the past, the United States' willingness to venture into the unknown means our idea of "authentic" isn't as firmly fixed as it is in countries with more deeply established cider traditions like England, France, or Spain. There are cider provocateurs all over the world, but some of the best are right here. But when does cider stop being cider? There's no agreed upon definition, at least not one we can quantify. I think if the soul of the drink remains apple—which leaves a huge range of possibilities—then it's still a cider.

The ciders in this chapter are in fact ciders. If a brewer can create an imperial sour mango milkshake IPA with lactose and goblin boogers and still call it beer, then a cider made with seaweed or tea leaves is most decidedly still a cider. (Any resemblance to actual beers, past, present, or future, is purely coincidental.)

Experimentation doesn't always indicate excess, so this chapter should primarily be considered a catch-all for ciders that don't fit even a loosely delineated official style definition rather than a collection of the extreme. They lean toward the gastronomical, the curious, and sometimes the oddball, not unlike the seasonally contentious pumpkin beers or even spicy pepper beers. They serve as beacons toward the fringes and the horizon of American cider, made by makers unfettered by tradition and looking to the future.

Botanist & Barrel //
Paw Paw Cider with Jasmine Tea
Cedar Grove, North Carolina | 6.9%

 North Carolina-based Botanist & Barrel are helping lead the new school cider charge with their co-ferments, pét-nat ciders, and other unconventional experiments that still pay homage to cider makers of yore. Their **Paw Paw Cider with Jasmine Tea**, a collaboration with kombucha maker Dalai Sofia, puts forth light and bright florals ranging from apple blossom to lavender and jasmine, all underscored with paw paw's unique fruit expression. While the fermented tea initially smooths out the spontaneous fermentation funk, a delicate complexity pleasantly emerges over time alongside a modest minerality and paw paw personality.

Paw paw fruit (sometimes spelled pawpaw) are the largest edible fruits indigenous to North America and are most commonly found in the Mid-Atlantic region and the southeastern United States. Its surprisingly tropical flavor tastes like a cross between a ripe banana and a fresh mango, and its soft flesh can be consumed raw or used in pudding, jams, ice cream, or, of course, cider! Here, the paw paw blends beautifully with the jasmine tea, resulting in a balanced yet elaborate drink that challenges the very definition of the segment.

Food Pairings

This unusual cider is unlike any other I've come across. Due to its light body, floral funk, and tropical flavor notes and aromatics, it's one of the more interesting ciders to pair with food. Its rustic nature would go well with a flaky galette overflowing with spring vegetables, any type of prepared mushrooms, pasta with fresh pesto, Parmesan cheese, or any other mild, hard cheese. For a taste of something sweet, snag a shortbread cookie or even try a paw paw dessert. Paw paw pudding is a common way to use this fascinating fruit, as is cheesecake or a fresh tart filled with paw paw jelly.

Ash & Elm Cider Company // Autumntide

Indianapolis, Indiana | 6.4%

 Every year, the same pumpkin spice debate rages on. Every year, I say the same thing: Drink what you like and tell any naysayers to kick rocks. But whichever side of the never-ending battle you fall on, pumpkin spice is here to stay, and there are plenty of pumpkin beer lovers who are sure to enjoy an apple-y substitute in **Autumntide**.

This light-bodied, pale gold, perfectly clear cider explodes with cinnamon, allspice, and cloves in the aroma as well as the flavor, all wrapped up neatly with a semisweet finish. This seasonal release is only available during autumn months, so keep your eyes peeled for this festive offering before it's gone. Ash & Elm also experiments with variations that include additions like cranberries, cold brew coffee, fig, and vanilla, and even include barrel-aging with maple and orange zest. It's all the best parts of fall, just waiting for you to come sip and enjoy with a piping hot bowl of chili and some good conversation.

About Ash & Elm

Indiana isn't known as a cider state—yet. But Ash & Elm founders Aaron and Andréa Homoya hope to build a cider movement in their own backyard using Aaron's background in beer to educate cider converts and sourcing local ingredients whenever possible, as well as giving back to causes that directly benefit their local community. Their taproom's variety of offerings ranges from standard (Dry) to seasonal (Autumntide) to specialty (Fickle Flame), and even include the occasional beer and cider collab, like a Dopplebock infused with local apple juice made in partnership with Indianapolis-based Kismetic Beer Company. Their cider subscription service, the A&E Cider Club, also allows fans from near and far to sample ciders either monthly or quarterly, making it easy to get your hands on Ash & Elm's best and brightest without much effort.

The Beer Lover's Guide to Cider

Cidergeist // Snug
Cincinnati, Ohio | 5.0%

 If adults ever got a snow day, **Snug** would be the cider to drink clad in flannel pajamas while watching through the window as snowflakes fall. This winter seasonal cider incorporates a five-spice blend of star anise, cinnamon, black peppercorn, clove, and fennel for a light-bodied, semidry, sessionable cider that's less filling than holiday beers like Winter Warmers or Christmas Ales, but just as festive.

Star anise initially dominates the aromatics, followed by the rest of the spices in a way reminiscent of mulled cider or a fresh-baked apple pie. Its low alcohol content allows drinkers to sip comfortably and even pair with more filling food, like a traditional turkey dinner or pot roast. However, the five-spice blend's inspiration comes directly from Chinese and Vietnamese cooking traditions, so I also recommend trying Snug with a steaming bowl of pho to accentuate the intricacies of both, or try it alongside your favorite Sichuan meal. I'm particularly partial to the mouth-numbing perfection of Sichuan saliva chicken, whose quirky moniker is a reference to its deliciousness. It's so good it'll make your mouth water—just like Snug.

About Cidergeist

Cidergeist is the cider offshoot of Rhinegeist Brewery; in addition to brewing beer and making cider, they also offer hard teas, as well as a line of canned fermented beverages that fall somewhere between craft beer and hard seltzer. Their malt base and real fruit concoctions fall squarely within the emerging wave of in-between beverages that are difficult to categorize. This anti-specialization approach allows businesses to diversify their offerings and attract a wider pool of inquisitive drinkers to satiate a wider variety of palates—just another example of how American cider pulls from other segments to thrive.

Tumbling Creek Cider Company //
Whiskey Barrel Aged Smoked Apple
Abingdon, Virginia | 7.5%

Rauchbiers, or beers with noticeable smoke characteristics, tend to be an acquired taste for most beer drinkers. But those with a predilection for this smoky style are likely to savor Tumbling Creek's small batch **Whiskey Barrel Aged Smoked Apple** cider. This cider's deft application of applewood smoked apples into a semidry cider, which is then aged over locally sourced whiskey barrels, culminates as a balanced, surprisingly delicate, and medium-bodied cider perfect for the smoky beer lover.

This particular interpretation of cider comes across with more wood and whiskey notes than phenolic imbalance—a tricky feat when it comes to any smoked beverage. Not all smoke-forward beverages manage to appeal to even the most adventurous consumers. In fact, few of them do. But Tumbling Creek has accomplished something remarkable with this particular product: creating a complex and unique cider that won't appeal to *everyone*, but promises to be someone's favorite.

Food Pairings

This particular cider goes beautifully with a thick slab of cedar plank salmon marinated in olive oil, lemon, garlic, salt, pepper, and dill, then grilled to perfection. Light smoke notes from both mesh gracefully together for an impressive spread that takes relatively little effort. Pizza lovers should also consider pairing with dill pickle pizza (yes, really), for as much as beer fans need to be convinced of Rauchbier's appeal at first, pickle pizza fans face the same hurdles. Gluten-free dough can be found with ease nowadays, and the creamy dill sauce, mozzarella and Parmesan cheeses, crunchy pickle slices, and generous helping of garlic atop a crispy crust might also convince the skeptics that trying something a little outrageous can result in the thrill of something new.

Treehorn Cider // Airing of Grievances
Marietta, Georgia | 5.9%

 As one of Georgia's small handful of craft cideries, Treehorn Cider takes its duty as regional cider diplomat seriously. From a flagship Dry for the traditionalists to a three-chili-infused cider for the heat seekers to a cider infused with miso and shiitake mushrooms for umami heads, their portfolio of products ranges from approachable to avant-garde, showing drinkers a brave new world of possibilities across a range of ciders.

Their winter seasonal, **Airing of Grievances**, packs a festivus punch with an enticingly spicy aroma full of tart cranberry, holiday spices, and fresh lemon pith. Even with so many assertive flavors, Airing of Grievances keeps itself in check with a light-to-moderate body and a crisp, clean, dry finish that manages to showcase each element without muddling them together. Everything pops on the tongue, but nothing pushes anything else out of the way. Bring a few cans to share as a holiday treat and watch as even the grinchiest drinker experiences a moment of illumination where their palate grows three sizes.

Food Pairings & Additional Recommendation

 A little ginger goes a long way, but Treehorn's **Ginger Reserve** manages to utilize the ancient root with restraint to create excellent results. This 5.9 percent core offering is as bold on its own as it is complementary with food and in cocktails, with huge amounts of ginger aromatics and smooth ginger flavor rounded off by apple juiciness. Treehorn recommends pairing it with Thai curry or chicken tikka masala, or mixing it to create a "Marietta Mule" (their take on a Moscow Mule). The option of simply splashing in some bourbon is always a good idea, but overall, it remains an educational example of cider's malleability.

Hemly Cider // Butterfly Lemonade
Courtland, California | 5.5%

From bright green cocktails to glitter beer, eye-catching drinks can be fun *and* delicious. One such striking example is **Butterfly Lemonade**, an amethyst-hued summer seasonal cider with a bit of a cult following. Not only is the bright color a great conversation starter, but the flavor of the liquid itself conjures up memories of a summertime Shandy, the bubbly blend of lager and lemon or lime soda ideal for quenching one's thirst on a hot afternoon.

To achieve the signature purple color, Hemly steeps a base cider made of California-grown apples and Meyer lemons in butterfly pea flowers, resulting in an unfiltered, light-bodied, swirly violet, relatively sweet cider packed with citrus fruit and floral notes throughout. Yes, it finishes sweeter than most beers, even Shandies or Radlers. Still, Butterfly Lemonade provides a fun and complex alternative for drinkers who enjoy light, summery beers with plenty of personality to go along with refreshment. This is one cider that is best enjoyed in a clean, clear glass rather than the can.

Notes About Perry

Perry is more commonly found across Europe than the United States. Pear trees grow slowly, are susceptible to disease, and bear less fruit than apple trees, and the fruit they do bear is delicate and easily bruised. In short, perries are a huge pain to make (thus their rarity), but a good perry is as delightful as it is elusive. Intrepid cider makers like Hemly have helped introduce the style to craft enthusiasts in the US, slowly but surely. The majority of Hemly's products are pear-based—Butterfly Lemonade being one exception—and use estate-grown fruit from their 165-year-old farm that goes back six generations.

Hemly Cider // Daybreak
Courtland, California | 6.0%

 Collaborations are common in beer and cider, but a cider maker collaborating with seaweed farmers? That's a first for me. **Daybreak** uses sustainably grown and harvested Pacific Ocean seaweed provided by Daybreak Seaweed, a women-owned co-op of regenerative seaweed farmers who support "food-focused climate solutions," according to their website. This partnership between Daybreak and Hemly blossomed in the early days of the COVID-19 pandemic lockdowns, going on to combine three types of seaweed to create an umami-centric pear cider with mellow aromatics and a light sweetness, all bolstered with a bite of brine throughout its delicate body. It's also one that cellars well, according to Hemly's director of events Rachael Levine. "We loved it when it was first released but are finding that as it ages, it gets even better," she explains.

Pears contain a naturally occurring, non-fermentable sugar called sorbitol, which results in a higher level of residual sugar after fermentation than apples. This gives perries and pear-based ciders a signature sweetness and round mouthfeel—ideal counterweights to seaweed's underlying salinity. Daybreak isn't salty, but it echoes that same balance of light body and a restrained pinch of salt found in world-class Goses. Hemly says Daybreak isn't currently scheduled for rerelease, but I'm holding out hope this unique creation reappears, or that someone else finds inspiration to attempt their own unusual experiments.

About Hemly Cider

Hemly is the sole maker in this book to earn two spotlights within one chapter, and they've earned it. The people behind Hemly also have roots in craft beer as both consumers and professionals, allowing them distinct insight into how to craft beverages that appeal to open-minded palates. Their ciders, both apple-based and pear-based, are available for local pickup at their Sacramento-area cider house (The Hangar), as well as from various retailers across Central and Northern California plus direct shipping from the maker to 39 states and Washington, DC.

UrbanTree Cidery // Sweet Heat Haze
Atlanta, Georgia | 6.5%

 Seeking out and savoring spicy foods and drinks is less of a learning curve and more of a birthright. With practice, those who hunger for heat can build a tolerance for it, learning to not just live with feeling the burn, but truly love it. For those early on their spice journey, UrbanTree Cidery's **Sweet Heat Haze** can serve as a starting point thanks to its generous pepper flavor, moderate pepper heat, and occasionally lower ABV (ranging from 5.0 percent to 6.5 percent in different batches).

In all batches, this ginger cider infused with habanero pepper zest starts strong with heavy habanero and apple on the nose and ginger notes arriving soon after. The body and flavor manage to pull off a surprising balance between all the ingredients, with the peppers providing more flavor than burn. This deviation from expectation reminds me of how differently hops present in cider versus beer. Wherever you personally stand with regards to spiciness, Sweet Heat Haze is an interesting opportunity to examine how ingredients like habaneros express themselves across a span of beverages.

Additional Recommendation

 Looking for something more extreme? Asheville, North Carolina-based Urban Orchard Cider Company's **Sidra Del Diablo** is not for the faint of heart or tongue. After opening, sniff with caution. I unfortunately did not, and my nose practically exploded with the intensity. By incorporating habanero with vanilla, Urban Orchard manages to restrain the harsh heat, making it an integral part of a light-bodied yet outrageously out-there cider well-suited for those searching for Scoville.

Vander Mill // Totally Roasted
Grand Rapids, Michigan | 6.5%

Totally Roasted starts with a traditional cider base of Michigan apples, but takes it to another level by infusing cinnamon, vanilla, and house-roasted pecans for a balanced finish falling between dry and sweet. The mild aroma teases at what's to come: a cider that keeps apples at the forefront but fills itself out with a hint of cinnamon and sugar and a hefty helping of toasted pecans (144 pounds of them per batch, to be precise). The painstakingly hands-on process for creating Totally Roasted requires meticulous and ongoing attention by its makers, and that level of TLC shines through in every roasty sip.

It's also available as a barrel-aged version, giving it an increased depth of complexity that still manages to refresh. Fans of malty or spiced cold weather beverages such as toasty Autumn Seasonal Beers, Winter Seasonal Beers, or Specialty Spice Beers can instead reach for Totally Roasted for a gluten-free selection that still furnishes plenty of festive flavor.

Food Pairings

Vander Mill owner Paul Vander Heide recommends pairing Totally Roasted with a winter salad of beets, squash, and soft cheese, thanks to the cider's "great cinnamon and vanilla backbone with a bright palate cleansing finish." For the barrel-aged version, he suggests something a little more substantial: a barbecue pulled pork sandwich to complement the big flavor and complexity of this robust cider option.

Stem Ciders // Leaves

Lafayette and Denver, Colorado | 4.2%

Ciders and perries earn a "botanical" designation with the addition of plant-based ingredients such as flowers, herbs, or spices.[35] Many ciders mentioned in this book fall under that wide-ranging group, but Stem Ciders' **Leaves** is perhaps the most thorough encapsulation of the concept.

Made with fresh-pressed apples, organic lemongrass, lemon verbena, and stevia leaf, this dry cider is infused with oolong and Chinese black fanning teas for an earthy, lemony fresh, lightly tart character with zero grams of sugar and 100 calories per 12-ounce can. Stem compares it to an Arnold Palmer, and while it's certainly as refreshing as the non-alcoholic summertime classic, Leaves steps up the complexity with huge tea notes and vivid citrus on the nose. Its flavor kicks off with an enjoyable tannic astringency from both the apples and tea blend that finishes smoothly, a little sweet, and skillfully balanced between the fruit and each botanical. Stem Ciders director Patrick Combs reveals that Leaves went through 16 different versions before they settled on the final recipe. I think it's safe to say they nailed it.

---

35   These could include ginger, cinnamon, rosemary, hops, roses, lavender, tea...the list goes on.

Food Pairings

Arnold Palmers are the ideal beverage for that ravenous period following summertime activities like swimming, golf, or beach volleyball. Likewise, Leaves goes well with casual picnic fare like sandwiches with chips, French fries, and of course a crunchy dill pickle spear. Club sandwiches, chicken salad, Caesar salad wraps, Cobb salads...apparently, if it starts with a C, it goes with Leaves. Combs also recommends pairing Leaves with leaves: salad, that is. "It goes really well with any type of salad, especially if it has an herbaceous vinaigrette," he explains. "The lemongrass notes are also super amicable to a bread course with dipping oils and vinegars."

Ciders for the Cider Lover

08

Ten Ciders for the Joy of Drinking Cider

Congratulations—you are now well on your way toward becoming a bona fide cider geek. That means the time has come to start drinking, understanding, and exploring cider for cider's sake, outside the realm of beer. Comparing cider to beer only gets you so far, and the ciders in this chapter are as far from beer as mezcal is from Riesling. As you continue your cider exploration, you may find yourself reverting to your beer knowledge. That's completely fine. However, these ciders are for when you're ready to leave beer behind and forge a new palate path wholly dedicated to cider.

During the tasting and research process for this book, I found myself calling certain products "cider ciders," which I define somewhat loosely: These achieve a high level of quality and complexity without any discernible callback to craft beer. The ciders in this chapter—and many more—celebrate apples in their own right and should be appreciated using a cider framework, nascent as it may be. When they are left to look inward, these ciders have the ability to provide a glimpse into the universal.

Since there are very few apples that contain the ideal levels of acid, tannins, and sugar to achieve cider's ultimate mission of balance all by themselves, cider makers often blend a number of apple varieties together to showcase the best characteristics of each and minimize less desirable attributes. However, single varietal ciders provide an invaluable opportunity to appreciate specific apples in their entirety, sharpening your ability to identify certain aspects of popular single variety cider apples such as Dabinett, Kingston Black, or

Yarlington Mill. SMaSH beers (Single Malt and Single Hop) also follow this philosophy, giving beer drinkers a chance to form a basis of opinion by analyzing specific malts and hops without multiple influences.

Plenty of blended ciders fall under the "cider for the cider lover" category, but there's a higher percentage of single variety ciders included here for these unique characteristics. Plus, terroir's dominion only goes so far. Yes, a Newtown Pippin grown in the glacial soils of New York will taste different than one grown in the Pamunkey soils of Virginia, but it will always retain the heart of a Newtown Pippin. Moving from blends to single varietals to comparing single varietals grown and made in vastly different geographical areas is a phenomenal path for the eager cider student to pursue. The ciders mentioned here can act as your guide.

Haykin Family Cider //
Kingston Black Reserve (2019)
Aurora, Colorado | 6.7%

 Haykin Family Cider has managed to find equal footing between embracing wine's elevated status and promoting cider's approachability, resulting in products that both wine experts and unschooled cider drinkers can easily recognize as exceptional. Bottled in 2019, Haykin's **Kingston Black Reserve** gives drinkers an opportunity to examine the English bittersharp variety from every angle.

In this case, its rich golden color, characteristically sweet and deceptively hot aromatics, flavors of fig, raisin, and other dark fruits, along with baked apple and pronounced tannins, culminating in a balanced finish between sweet and dry allow consumers of all expertise levels to contemplate the beauty of this celebrated cider apple. While its high carbonation and attenuation recall stronger Belgian beer styles that similarly evoke notes of dark candied fruits, and its sparkling personality and fruit-forward nature reflect a winemaker's sensibility, Haykin's Kingston Black Reserve remains first and foremost a classic example of a true cider lover's cider.

About Haykin Family Cider

Cider is vast and varied enough to warrant its own category. However, the reality remains that most American consumers aren't versed well enough in cider's particular qualities for it to exist as a singularity—yet. As that eventuality continues to take shape, cider makers like Haykin continue to help drinkers tiptoe their way towards cider by using familiar cues like glassware.

Haykin co-founder and CEO Talia Haykin explains they intentionally use tulip glasses in their tasting room to provide a touchpoint for potential converts. "We like the bulbousness of the glass for aroma and flavor, but we thought a flute would be too hard for the folks who aren't wine drinkers," she says. It's a thoughtful touch that will help convince spirits, beer, and wine drinkers to give cider a try.

Western Cider // Ranch Hand
Missoula, Montana | 6.5%

 Cider can be as fancy as Champagne and as down-to-earth as a macro Lager. This ubiquitousness is one of cider's greatest strengths, and something Western Cider has tapped into with its consistently approachable creations.

Made with 100 percent Northwest apples, **Ranch Hand** uses two yeast strains to simulate wild fermentation, all while keeping it under the cider maker's control. Within its light body lies big flavor ranging from honey and juicy apple to light cherry and fresh baking dough. Finishing mostly dry, this crystal-clear, moderately carbonated, mildly aromatic cider emulates the easygoing nature of a craft lager while simultaneously defining itself as nothing but what it is: the fermented juice of apples, carefully picked, pressed, and crafted into a taste of American terroir.

Food Pairings

Western describes Ranch Hand as "reliable and sturdy." I call it the ideal pairing with comfort food. A piled-high Reuben, meatball sub, or even a grilled cheese sandwich (made as fancy or as simple as you please) are all hearty enough to stand up to this cider's universal appeal. For those looking to test the wide-ranging promise of a cider "that works anywhere," Ranch Hand can be just as at home with a sandwich as it is alongside a fancy spread. Its light body and subtle fruit notes pop next to savory caviar spreads and aged cheese, as well as umami-packed options like seaweed salad, *cánh gà chiên nước mắm*,[36] or even a snack of popcorn sprinkled with nutritional yeast. Crack a can of Ranch Hand at your next picnic or potluck and see if there's anything it *doesn't* go with—my guess is no.

---

36 Vietnamese fish sauce-glazed chicken wings.

Raging Cider & Mead Company // Hyslop Single Varietal (2019)

San Marcos, California | 6.0%

Raging Cider is known more for offbeat creativity than consistency. Head cider maker Dave Carr combines English cider tradition with a hyperlocal focus by using only San Diego County-grown fruit as well as native yeasts, resulting in a hugely varied portfolio of products ranging from single varietal ciders to pommeaus, perries, English scrumpys,[37] jerkums,[38] and other esoteric experiments that test even seasoned cider fans' palates. If you're up for it, a great place to start is with their **Hyslop Single Varietal**, made with early harvested crabapples which are barrel-fermented and then aged on lees for one year.

The result is a highly acidic, structured, and somewhat chewy cider packed with barrel aroma and flavor that leans toward leather and tannins. Its finishing complexity (one that carries over residual sweetness yet remains balanced), deep orange-gold color, and full body resemble certain Belgian beer styles. However, thanks to its rich apple backbone, this challenging but compelling cider provides a standout look at a classic cider crabapple.

Apples in California

As one of the top five apple producing states in the United States, California's annual output stands at a precipice due to a number of factors. First, the increasing cost and scarcity of both farmland and water make it more difficult than ever for farmers. Secondly, rising temperatures due to climate change reduce the number of apple varieties that can withstand hotter days and warmer nights. Finally, as the second largest domestic exporter of apples,

---

37 Strong, tannic, unfiltered cider often served still.
38 An alcoholic drink made from the fermented juice of plums.

California has to compete with international growers from other countries, including China, which is by far the largest apple producer in the world. But with dedicated orchardists and cider makers like Raging Cider continuing to nurture new generations of cider lovers, California's local terroir stands a great chance at not just surviving, but thriving.

Virtue Cider // Old Spot (2021)
Fennville, Michigan | 7.8%

 Named for the distinctively spotted orchard pigs of Gloucestershire, England, **Old Spot** blends British folklore with American cider heritage to create a light-bodied, unfiltered, somewhat floral, and mildly funky beverage that captures the pastoral simplicity of the English countryside. Like many British styles, this still English pub cider focuses more on flavor and mouthfeel than effervescence, giving its barrel-aged qualities an unobstructed canvas on which to shine.

Even at nearly 8.0 percent ABV, Old Spot finishes smooth, bright, and mostly dry, with hints of vanilla tempering the wood barrel expression while keeping juicy apple notes as the focus. Its fresh farmhouse flavor bursts with complexity as well as approachability, making it a fitting choice for anyone looking for a true cider's cider.

Old Spot is available over a number of vintages, including 2019 (8.2 percent) and the aforementioned 2021, so keep an eye out for future releases to put together a vertical flight tasting. As with beer, when aging cider, it's best to find a cool, dark room with consistent temperature like a basement, closet, or cellar. Bottle conditioned ciders are still developing their personality, so they're generally suited for cellaring, as are unpasteurized or barrel-aged ciders, which can mature in complexity over time. Typically, canned cider and beer should be consumed right away. Of course, if any label specifically states to drink as fresh as possible, it's always best to defer to the cider maker's guidance.

Maintain the British-American alliance by pairing Old Spot with British pub fare such as fish and chips or Scotch eggs. A more on-the-nose pairing might be roast pork loin with baked apples, but only if you wish to keep things literal. Virtue recommends pairing it with a meat pie or sharp cheddar, and I'll add some pungent soft cheeses to the list as well, like Époisses or Murray's Cave Aged Reserve Greensward, an aged Vermont cheese washed in cider.

Snow Capped Cider // Gold Rush
Cedaredge, Colorado | 6.9%

 There are a few ways to experience the unique taste of the Rocky Mountains, but I prefer to reach for a gold can with burgundy mountains for the best expression of the Western Slope's terroir. Heritage apples used in Snow Capped's **Gold Rush** are grown at 6,130 feet elevation, one of the highest elevation orchards in the world, according to owner and head cider maker Kari Williams.

This gives the English and French varieties an inimitable regional character full of luscious and balanced sweetness, medium mouthfeel, and plenty of bubbles. The blend of Blanc Mollet, Ashmead's Kernel, Golden Russet, and Dabinett apples meld together to deliver an easy-drinking cider with bright baked apple aromas and flavors that finish a tad sweet, but refreshing and consistent.

Food Pairings

Snow Capped recommends pairing Gold Rush with savory and seasonal dishes, such as roasted fall vegetables, to bring out the cider's sweetness. Of course, cheese remains a prevalent option for virtually every cider. This one is no exception, with Cheddar, Brie, and Camembert topping the list. Gold Rush also complements hearty entrees like Filipino chicken adobo, *congee*,[39] lasagna, chili, or short ribs—any cozy cold weather meal works well with this mountain-made beverage.

Gluten-free pairing ideas include stuffed bell peppers, portobello mushroom "steaks," or one of my fast and easy go-tos: sheet pan baked eggs atop a bed of kale and sprinkled with goat cheese. Personally, I think this cider works as well as a brunch beverage as it does at dinner, so consider trying it with a classic Denver omelet, corned beef hash, or *ube pandesal*[40] to start your day deliciously.

---

39   A common Chinese comfort food, this thick, silky rice porridge can be made with chicken stock, ginger, green onions, poached eggs, or any other accoutrements you'd like.

40   Sweet, pillowy, and bright purple Filipino bread rolls. The vibrant hue comes from *ube*, a purple root vegetable native to Southeast Asia.

Island Orchard Cider //
Oak Aged Apple Cider

Ellison Bay, Wisconsin | 6.9%

 Some ciders begin to really shine after they've warmed up a bit, and **Oak Aged Apple Cider** is one such example. This dry-finishing cider ages on oak for at least three months before finishing, giving it a layered texture that starts with a moderate baking spice aroma and matures toward a full-bodied, rich apple depth with a very light suggestion of woodiness.

No alcohol warmth or astringency lingers on the finish, which instead culminates in a juicy, dry, straightforward cider centering around a medley of apples for a balanced expression. Its simplistic approach ensures that the apples themselves remain the stars of the show, but the blend's composition manages to highlight the best attributes of each variety. Oak Aged Apple Cider meshes approachability and artistry in the best ways, showcasing the range of pome fruit in a single glass.

About Island Orchard Cider

Located on the tip of Wisconsin's Door Peninsula, Island Orchard uses fruit ferried over from nearby Washington Island to create their terroir-laden ciders and vinegars. Owners Yannique and Bob Purman compare the similarly cool and somewhat humid climate along Lake Michigan to another renowned cider region: Normandy, France. While Wisconsin cider has a ways to travel to achieve the notoriety of *cidre de Normandie*,[41] as long as growers and producers like Island Orchard continue to nurture the burgeoning demand for classical ciders made with care, there's no telling where the industry can go.

---

41 Cider from Normandy, France. Apples grown in Normandy tend to have low acid with high levels of tannins and pectins, making them prime varieties for *keeving*. Keeving is a natural method of fermentation that prevents yeast from fully fermenting in order to leave some residual sugar. The results are sparkling ciders that range from semidry to sweet without any back-sweetening.

Old Town Cidery // Pearsecco
Winchester, Virginia | 6.9%

 As fourth-generation fruit farmers in the Shenandoah Valley of northwestern Virginia, the Glaize family only uses apples they grow to make cider at Old Town. "A good cider starts with the right apple," says David Glaize, who co-owns Old Town Cidery with his brother Philip. In **Pearsecco**'s case, it's the right apples and pears, the latter of which are currently sourced from a neighboring farm. "We have planted our own pear trees for future batches," he promises.

To create Pearsecco, cider maker Stephen Kelly first presses and blends GoldRush, York, Greening, and other apple varieties and ferments the juice to a dry-finishing base cider. Using the same apple press, he then pulverizes the Virginia-grown Asian pears and adds the juice to the base cider for a mild, inviting, and clean-finishing spin on a perry. With light florals and honeycomb on the nose followed by a light body that is moderately carbonated with a mostly dry finish, this is one of Old Town's best. It's "definitely a fan favorite," says Glaize.

Food Pairings

With pear providing a light sweetness and round finish to the crisp apple base, Glaize says Pearsecco pairs beautifully with braised pork roast with roasted vegetables. "And of course, an apple chutney on top of the pork," he adds. He also suggests swapping a can of Pearsecco to use for a beer can chicken-turned-cider can chicken—with one suggestion. "Make sure you remove the sleeved wrap on the can first!" he laughs.

Finger Lakes Cider House // Baldwin
Interlaken, New York | 8.4%

The first time I tried **Baldwin** from Finger Lakes Cider House, I found myself wishing I was on a picnic near a river, eating a fresh croissant smothered in salted butter and washing it down with this ultra-dry, ultra-bubbly cider packed with minerality and lemon notes on the finish. Unfortunately, I was just in my kitchen, but this single varietal cider has a magically transporting quality. It tastes of apples, yes, but also of earth, of spring, of liquid spilling over ancient rocks into a silver goblet as an invigorating elixir straight from the orchard.

Once considered the most popular apple of the Northeast, the popularity of Baldwins waned after a catastrophic freeze in 1934. Over recent years, this versatile variety has begun a steady rebound and is once again being used by some American cideries. I recommend pairing Baldwin with unfussy dishes made with high-end ingredients: fresh bread, hard cheese, or a just-baked blueberry scone.

Additional Recommendations

It's nearly impossible to pick a single favorite from Finger Lakes Cider House's substantial cider portfolio, so I'm not even going to try. Additional standouts include **Funkhouse** and **Pioneer Pippin**. Both are 8.4 percent ABV, both are made using the traditional method, and both are hand-disgorged, which is an extremely precise (and nerve-wracking) technique that occurs after secondary fermentation. It involves popping a bottle's cap off at exactly the right time to get rid of the lees left in the neck of an inverted bottle *without* losing a lot of

The Beer Lover's Guide to Cider

cider in the process. It's difficult to accomplish, but results in extremely clear and super bubbly cider that retains its complexity without any gunk.

Funkhouse leans more toward a farmhouse-style cider with huge, rich aromatics, while Pioneer Pippin's crab apple blend balances high acid with a juicy semidry finish. Both are restrained in all the right ways and highly expressive throughout, resulting in a win-win-win for whatever ciders you choose. (Like many cideries, the alcohol content of some Finger Lakes Cider House ciders tends to fluctuate year by year.)

Eden Specialty Ciders // Brut Nature
Newport, Vermont | 8.0%

Champagne may be the most famous product made with the traditional method,[42] but the sparkling French white wine faces competition from the cider world with alternatives like **Brut Nature**. This bone dry and naturally sparkling cider begins by first fermenting a cider base of heirloom and bittersweet apples in stainless steel, then adds a splash of high-sugar and high-alcohol ice cider to prompt secondary fermentation in bottles. After resting for at least a year and a half, Eden hand-disgorges each bottle, resulting in a wildly complex, extremely dry, very effervescent cider with a touch of horse blanket, aged apple, and rustic farmhouse charm.

I've seen vintages with a slightly higher alcohol content (8.4 percent versus 8.0 percent), but it's all in the ballpark, and when producers like Eden work with blends containing a large number of apple varieties (Brut Nature has at least 14), absolute consistency isn't the point. The soul of this cider remains the same year after year, even if the product itself unfurls a bit differently. It's an exciting surprise each and every time, but the only thing unsurprising is the quality and care taken with each batch.

Food Pairings

Like Champagne, Brut Nature is a fabulously versatile beverage to pair with food. The biggest question you should ask yourself is simply: What are you in the mood for? Oysters? A medium rare ribeye steak with grilled asparagus and buttery potatoes? A macaron (or two)? The sky's the limit with this cider, which is a no-brainer to pop open anytime. Whether you're home alone watching a movie or entertaining friends at a cocktail party, when you reach for Brut Nature, you're guaranteed to have a good time.

---

42 A creation method that specifies a primary fermentation followed by a secondary fermentation in the bottle before disgorgement, resulting in no residual sugar. In some instances, a cider maker may "dose" the final bottle by adding a small amount of liquid sugar to balance an ultra-dry finish and fill the bottle completely, as some liquid may be lost during disgorgement.

Dragon's Head Cider // Bittersweet
Vashon Island, Washington | 7.3%

Using nothing but apples is the Dragon's Head way of doing things, and it's working out well for them. Located on Vashon Island in Puget Sound, just a short ferry ride from Seattle and Tacoma, Dragon's Head Cider makes traditional cider with a craftsman's touch. Their method of hands-on picking, pressing, and bottling—mostly using apples from their own orchard—means it's unlikely they'll ever grow much bigger than they are, but that's part of the shifting seasonal magic of cider.

With that temperamental terroir in mind, expect every bottling of **Bittersweet** to be ever so slightly different thanks to varying weather patterns and events that affect the fruit of each year's harvest. But at its heart, Bittersweet remains an ideal example of mixing American-grown English and French cider apples into a symphonic blend carefully balanced for a rich, golden cider high in tannins and low in acid. Somehow, even after using over twenty apple varieties to create this extraordinarily complex, full-bodied beverage, Dragon's Head manages to capture pure pleasure and bottle it for our enjoyment.

Additional Recommendation

What Dragon's Head lacks in naming creativity, they more than make up for in artistry, as evidenced by their **Wild Fermented** cider. This 6.9 percent cider has everything the cider lover could want: elaborate aromatics, a light but balanced barnyard funkiness, and an apple-centric base that promotes tannins for a lush body and dry finish. Anyone who desires to begin appreciating cider as the truly incomparable beverage it is need only look to Dragon's Head for a suitable starting line.

Conclusion

Humans are further removed from farms and fields than we ever have been throughout the course of history. Demand for immediate gratification and convenience at a low cost has fundamentally changed our relationship with the food and drink we put into our bodies.

Exploring cider means taking one small step toward reestablishing our connection with the earth. This doesn't mean it's better for you in terms of being a magical panacea of wellness. It's just one way we as a species can reconnect with the bounty of nature and realize what we've been missing. It's possible to tap into that instinct through beer, but cider simply lies that much closer to its origins.

Right now, there aren't enough apple trees growing across the United States to meet cider's potential. Even if we planted hundreds of thousands more trees today, it would take years to bear enough fruit for the industry to fully emerge as a viable, sustainable, competitive segment. So what can we do?

Protect farmland, fight climate change, support farmers and agricultural workers, and yes, drink cider. The best time to plant a tree is 50 years ago, but the second-best time is right now. If we establish a strong foundation today to support tomorrow's demand, future generations of cider lovers will be able to experience fresh craft cider anywhere in the country and develop an iconic American craft cider culture rivaling those of Spain, France, Germany, and the UK. The coming waves of new cider lovers are our strength, and the knowledge you've gleaned here is a crucial part of it.

Beer has very little to teach cider. In fact, beer could learn quite a bit about said nature of humanity, as well as about nature itself, if it took a few lessons from cider. But cider occupies a unique position, able to observe the stratospheric rise and eventual leveling out of the beer industry and adjust accordingly. I believe if people are allowed—nay, encouraged—to use beer as a jumping-off point in order to draw parallels of recognition in a new-to-you beverage, even the tiniest foothold may allow them to scale the mountain of discovery.

Should you choose to continue your cider journey, begin drinking what you can get locally or travel to find more. Start trying things, connecting styles, and learning about cider makers. Walk into a bottle shop or cider bar and start asking questions. What are this maker's values? Are their operations inclusive and ethical? Do they practice sustainability? Are they making the cider world—and the world in general—a better place? Compare American-made ciders to the keeved ciders of France, German apfelwein,[43] or an English scrumpy. There's a whole world of cider out there, and it's waiting for you.

I truly believe the more cider you drink, the more you'll love it. With experience comes appreciation, with appreciation comes knowledge, and with knowledge comes a desire to pass it on. Not one single person can claim a universal comprehension of cider. Rather, it's up to each one of us to add a single thread into cider's ever-growing tapestry, a rich history and ongoing pilgrimage being woven every day, season, year, and century. There is no apex of cider education to reach, no final test to mark one's arrival at the end. You simply keep exploring.

If you try a few ciders and decide to stick to beer, that's fine. But hopefully you walk away with an increased knowledge of your own palate, preferences, and place. That's never a waste of time. Drink what you want. I hope at least some of it is cider.

---

43   German for "cider"

The United States of Cider

In addition to the cideries already mentioned in these pages, here are some more cider makers, cider houses, cider bars, and bottle shops across the country to help launch your cider odyssey.

1. Absolem Cider - Winthrop, Maine

2. ACE Cider - Sebastopol, California

3. Alaska Ciderworks - Talkeetna, Alaska

4. Albemarle CiderWorks - North Garden, Virginia

5. Alma's Cider & Beer - Los Angeles, California

6. Alpenfire Cider - Port Townsend, Washington

7. Art+Science - Sheridan, Oregon

8. AVID Cider Company - Bend, Oregon

9. Benny Boy Brewing - Los Angeles, California

10. Bivouac Ciderworks - San Diego, California

11. Black Bear Cider Company - St. Louis, Missouri

12. Blake's Hard Cider - Armada, Michigan

13. Bløm Meadworks - Ann Arbor, Michigan

14. Blue Bee Cider - Richmond, Virginia

15. Brick River Cider Company - St. Louis, Missouri

16. Brooklyn Cider House - New Paltz, New York

17. Calico Cidery - Julian, California

18. Citizen Cider - Burlington, Vermont

19. The Craftroom - Albuquerque, New Mexico

20. Diskin Cider - Nashville, Tennessee

21. D.O.P.E. Cider House and Winery - Youngstown, Ohio

22. Double Shovel Cider Company - Anchorage, Alaska

23. Downeast Cider House - East Boston, Massachusetts

24. Embark Craft Ciderworks - Williamson, New York

25. ERIS Brewery & Cider House - Chicago, Illinois

26. Eve's Cidery - Van Etten, New York

27. Fable Farm Fermentory - Barnard, Vermont

28. Far From The Tree Cider - Salem, Massachusetts

29. Farmstead Cider - Jackson, Wyoming

30. Farnum Hill Ciders - Lebanon, New Hampshire

31. Finnriver Farm & Cidery - Chimacum, Washington

32. Flora & Ferment Ciderhouse - Albany, California

33. Green Bench Mead & Cider - St. Petersburg, Florida

34. Incline Cider - Tacoma, Washington

35. Ironbound Farm and Ciderhouse - Asbury, New Jersey

36. KC Cider Company - St. Joseph, Missouri

37. Kingfish Cider - Jefferson, Louisiana

38. La Familia Cider - Salem, Oregon

39. Lost Boy Cider - Alexandria, Virginia

40. Meriwether Cider Company - Garden City, Idaho

41. Milk & Honey Ciders - St. Joseph, Minnesota

42. Muse Cider Bar - Haydenville, Massachusetts

43. Newtopia Cyder - San Diego, California

44. The Northman Beer & Cider Garden - Chicago, Illinois

45. OK Cider - Oklahoma City, Oklahoma

46. Portersfield Cider - Pownal, Maine

47. Posterity Ciderworks - Mokelumne Hill, California

48. Ragged & Right Cider - Mount Vernon, Washington

49. Red Clay Ciderworks - Charlotte, North Carolina

50. Redbyrd Orchard Cider - Trumansburg, New York

51. Redfield Cider Bar & Bottle Shop - Oakland, California

52. Rose Hill Ferments - Red Hook, New York

53. Scion Cider Bar - Salt Lake City, Utah

54. Seattle Cider Company - Seattle, Washington

55. Serpentine Cider - San Diego, California

56. Ship's Wheel Hard Cider - North Charleston, South Carolina

57. Snowdrift Cider Company - East Wenatchee, Washington

58. South Hill Cider - Ithaca, New York

59. Swift Cider - Portland, Oregon

60. Tanuki Cider - Santa Cruz, California

61. Tieton Cider Works - Yakima, Washington

62. Tilted Shed Ciderworks - Windsor, California

The Beer Lover's Guide to Cider

63. Uncle John's Cider Mill - St. Johns, Michigan

64. Waves Cider Company - Columbia, Missouri

65. West County Cider - Shelburne Falls, Massachusetts

66. Wild Terra Cider - Fargo, North Dakota

67. Woodchuck Hard Cider - Middlebury, Vermont

68. Young American Hard Cider - Philadelphia, Pennsylvania

Resources

I encourage you to find and attend any of the numerous Cider Week celebrations across the country to immerse yourself in cider heaven. There are also various cider box subscriptions, bottle shops, websites, books, magazines, and other resources to continue learning. Whether you wish to know how to make your own cider, the history of apple cultivation across the world or colonial influence on North American orchards, American heirloom varieties, agricultural risks like fire blight and what to do about it, breeding and grafting, or any other aspect of cider, here are a few places to start.

Books

- *Cider Made Simple: All About Your New Favorite Drink* by Jeff Alworth (Chronicle Books, 2015)

- *Tasting Cider: The CIDERCRAFT® Guide to the Distinctive Flavors of North American Hard Cider* by Erin James and CIDERCRAFT Magazine (Storey Publishing, 2017)

- *American Cider: A Modern Guide to a Historic Beverage* by Dan Pucci and Craig Cavallo (Ballantine Books, 2021)

- *World's Best Ciders: Taste, Tradition, and Terroir* by Pete Brown and Bill Bradshaw (Union Square & Co., 2013)

- *Odd Apples* by William Mullan (Hatje Cantz, 2021)

- *The Cider Insider* by Susanna Forbes (Quadrille Publishing, 2019)

- *Uncultivated: Wild Apples, Real Cider, and the Complicated Art of Making a Living* by Andy Brennan (Chelsea Green Publishing, 2019)

- *Cider Revival: Dispatches from the Orchard* by Jason Wilson (Harry N. Abrams, 2019)

- *Ciderology: From History and Heritage to the Craft Cider Revolution* by Gabe Cook (Spruce, 2018)

- *Modern British Cider* by Gabe Cook (Campaign for Real Ale, 2021)

- *Fine Cider: Understanding the world of fine, natural cider* by Felix Nash (Dog 'n' Bone, 2019)

- *Apples of Uncommon Character: Heirlooms, Modern Classics, and Little-Known Wonders* by Rowan Jacobsen (Bloomsbury USA, 2014)

Additional Resources

- BJCP's "Introduction to Cider" Guidelines: bjcp.org/beer-styles/introduction-to-cider-guidelines

- ACA study materials to become a Certified Cider Professional or Certified Pommelier: ciderassociation.org/certification

- *Cider Review*: cider-review.com

- *Cidercraft Magazine*: cidercraftmag.com

- *Malus*, a quarterly print zine/Instagram page: @maluszine

- *Neutral Cider Hotel* podcast: neutralciderhotel.com

- *Cider Chat* podcast: ciderchat.com

- Northwest Cider Association's Cider Club: nwciderclub.com

Acknowledgments

First and foremost, thank you to my husband Ashton Ivey, who always allowed me time to write, and to my son Arthur, who did his best to occupy said time with games and crafts instead. (I'll admit I caved on more than one occasion.) Endless gratitude to my agent Kim Lindman at Stonesong and to my publisher Brenda Knight at Mango Publishing, who both championed this book into reality, and to Tim Skirven and Luke Schmuecker for creating the amazing visuals that brought this book to life.

Thanks to all the cider makers, writers, and experts from around the world who graciously shared their time and expertise with me, including but not limited to: Gabe Cook, Soham Bhatt, Albert Johnson, Susanna Forbes, Tom Oliver, Felix Nash, Greg Hall, Eleanor Leger, Nat West, Lauren Bloom, Colin Post, Sean Turley, Chris Shields, Garrett Oliver, Dave Carr, Ian Wright, Lara Worm, Sean Harris, Bill and Pauline Storum, and Michelle McGrath. Your insights shaped an idea into these pages—thank you. Additional thanks to every cider maker who sent me their products and trusted me to evaluate them as honestly as possible. I hope this book leads readers to you.

To all my writing and editing colleagues: Claire Bullen and Emma Janzen for their early and ongoing guidance; Bryan Roth, Lily Waite, and Kate Bernot for their ceaseless support; Pat Walls for his time spent carefully combing through the manuscript; Joshua Bernstein, Dr. J Jackson-Beckham, Joe Stange, Latiesha Cook, Bill Shufelt, Matt Brynildson, Jim Koch, and everyone who endorsed the book; and to my editors at *The Washington Post, SevenFifty Daily,* and *VinePair* for giving me the opportunity to write about cider leading up to this. Thank you also to the current BJCP President, Dennis Mitchell, for permitting me to reference the 2021 Beer Style Guidelines as the authoritative reference of both historical and evolving beer styles.

Thank you to those who helped me taste and evaluate my way through hundreds of ciders: Gene Fielden, George Thornton, Luke Schmuecker, Jessica Hicks, Daylen Dalrymple, Nickie Peña, and everyone else I had the privilege of sipping with, as well as Jeff Motch for letting me talk about and taste ciders in front of a crowd. Special thanks to Andy Hannas for bringing me into the worlds of cider *and* beer, and for being a first-class friend for 20 years (and counting).

Thank you to all of the cider enthusiasts across the world who have already started the cider revolution. Cheers to the future.

About the Forewordist

Jeff Alworth founded the award-winning blog *Beervana* in 2006. He is also the author of numerous books, including *Cider Made Simple, The Beer Bible, The Secrets of Master Brewers,* and *The Widmer Way.* He is based in Portland, Oregon.

About the Author

Beth Demmon is an award-winning writer whose work has appeared in publications like *The Washington Post, Civil Eats, Saveur Magazine, PUNCH, VinePair, Playboy, Food & Wine, Wine Enthusiast, VICE* and many more. She is the freelance drinks columnist at *San Diego Magazine* and regular podcast host for *Good Beer Hunting*. Her Substack newsletter *Prohibitchin'* aims to amplify diverse voices of people working in craft beer, spirits, cider, wine, and other beverage alcohol segments who don't often get the recognition they deserve. Beth is also a Certified Beer Judge through the Beer Judge Certification Program, a Certified Cider Professional through the American Cider Association, and a member of the North American Guild of Beer Writers. *The Beer Lover's Guide to Cider* is her first book. She lives in San Diego, California. Learn more at bethdemmon.com.

Mango Publishing, established in 2014, publishes an eclectic list of books by diverse authors—both new and established voices—on topics ranging from business, personal growth, women's empowerment, LGBTQ+ studies, health, and spirituality to history, popular culture, time management, decluttering, lifestyle, mental wellness, aging, and sustainable living. We were named 2019 *and* 2020's #1 fastest-growing independent publisher by *Publishers Weekly*. Our success is driven by our main goal, which is to publish high-quality books that will entertain readers as well as make a positive difference in their lives.

Our readers are our most important resource; we value your input, suggestions, and ideas. We'd love to hear from you—after all, we are publishing books for you!

Please stay in touch with us and follow us at:

Facebook: Mango Publishing
Twitter: @MangoPublishing
Instagram: @MangoPublishing
LinkedIn: Mango Publishing
Pinterest: Mango Publishing
Newsletter: mangopublishinggroup.com/newsletter

Join us on Mango's journey to reinvent publishing, one book at a time.